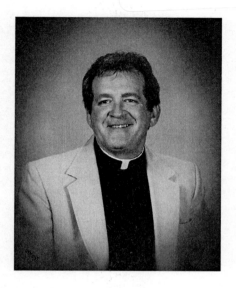

E.M. Dempsey is the eldest son of John N. Dempsey and Mary Frey Dempsey. He was born and raised in the small mill town of Putnam. CT. Starting at age fourteen, Ed studied for the priesthood in Connecticut, Rochester, New York, and lssy-les-Mounlineaux, France (a Parisian suburb). He was ordained a priest of the diocese of Norwich, CT in 1967. Although now retired, he continues with priestly duties in parishes on weekends and in giving retreats as invited. In his active days, Ed worked in the field of social services, principally as the Executive Director of a community – based behavioral health agency. In retirement, Ed has returned home to Connecticut's Quiet Corner and the village of North Woodstock.

To the memory of that immigrant kid arrived on these shores at the age of ten, who never forgot his beginnings and always revered and respected the opportunities afforded him by his new home, and who tried, throughout his life, to give back to the city and state and country that welcomed him and honored him with their confidence, and to her, without whom, by his admission, life would not have been worth the living, these memoirs are lovingly dedicated by an eldest son.

E.M. Dempsey

Remembering John Noel Dempsey: A Man Who Did Good

Austin Macauley Publishers™

LONDON • CAMBRIDGE • NEW YORK • SHARJAH

Ordering Information
Quantity sales: Special discounts are available on quantity purchases by corporations, associations, and others. For details, contact the publisher at the address below.

Publisher's Cataloging-in-Publication data
Dempsey, E.M.
Remembering John Noel Dempsey: A Man Who Did Good

ISBN 9781685629472 (Paperback)
ISBN 9781685629489 (Hardback)
ISBN 9781685629496 (ePub e-book)

Library of Congress Control Number: 2023907005

www.austinmacauley.com/us

First Published 2023
Austin Macauley Publishers LLC
40 Wall Street, 33rd Floor, Suite 3302
New York, NY 10005
USA

mail-usa@austinmacauley.com
+1 (646) 5125767

I am more than happy to acknowledge my sincere gratitude to:

My youngest brother, Kevin, for remembering and safeguarding the original dot-matrix printout of the first drafts of the text. Without his kindness in keeping and then giving back these pages, I would in all probability never have gone back and started over.

Connecticut's State Historian, Walter Woodward, whose encouragement and gentle persuasion were crucial to the completion.

The multiple people whose pieces of Dad's story are the 'stuff' of these recollections.

Charlie Morse, reporter, and political commentator extraordinaire, whose accompaniment through the years and across the globe came to have such meaning for our family.

The people of Putnam, Dad's home, then and now, who never seem to forget, and who, in countless ways, have enshrined and honored his memory.

Foreword

Charles F. J. Morse, the quintessential political analyst, and columnist wrote for The Hartford Courant for many years. Sadly, he died in 2020 before I had the good sense to ask that he write a foreword to these memoirs. Charlie had covered my father's days in office both in Connecticut and elsewhere. He knew my father well. He became a good friend not only to Dad but to our entire family as well. There might well be a lot of things that Charles Morse would have wanted to write as he looked back on Dad's public career. But his writer's acumen was never more obvious nor more 'spot on' than when his column, Political Insights, appeared in The Courant's edition on Monday, June 26, 1989. Dad was hospitalized and had recently been diagnosed with terminal small-cell lung cancer. Following Dad's death, Charlie would continue to write about Dad in Charlie's own inimitable, innately personal style. On this particular occasion, he chose to focus on his days covering Dad in a way that was totally Charlie's, a way never before or since imitated by another writer of whom I am aware. Let his column now serve as an apt and unique foreword to this book.

It is a good time to talk of John Dempsey – not as the governor or public servant or as a patient ill in the hospital that bears his name – but of the flair and fun of John Dempsey.

Nowadays, covering governors and senators and mayors has turned chilly, adversarial, reserved, made-for-television.

Covering John Dempsey was fun.

He is perhaps the last Connecticut governor and politician to be associated with the word.

The reasons are many and watching him and being with him made them apparent.

Watching him beam in the backseat of a sparkling, white convertible in downtown Hartford that afternoon in 1960 – in between Abraham Ribicoff, John F. Kennedy, and John M. Bailey – confetti pouring from the sky.

The governor's natural fondness for people extended to reporters. He remembered birthdays and anniversaries. He carried a few to their graves.

Watching him work the receiving lines of hundreds of people leading into his office on inauguration days was intriguing. Not only were last names remembered, but first names too – including kids.'

Sharing early morning card tables with him and governors of New England – perhaps John King of New Hampshire or John Chaffee of Rhode Island or John Volpe of Massachusetts, after conferences at Smugglers' Notch, VT, Boston, and Manchester, NH – jacks or better to open.

The routine – budgets and state-of-the-state messages, legislatures, ribbon-cuttings, speeches, fund-raisers, testimonials – fade into the past. What remains is fun.

Watching him, year after year, race handicapped children to the raft and back at Harkness Memorial State Park in Waterford. And watching him lose, year after year, to their squealing delight.

There was even an element of fun in the unfunny.

Watching the state police cruiser, lights flashing bear down on the governor's limousine as it headed west on the Massachusetts Turnpike, and anticipating a speeding pinch.

Instead, it was the word that President Kennedy had been shot in Dallas.

In a maintenance garage just off the turnpike, the governor learned of Kennedy's death from a beat-up radio with missing dials.

Sharing one magical week in Ireland in 1965 when John Dempsey returned to Cahir, the town of his birth and boyhood, as the only Irish-born governor of an American state.

Dictating daily stories by Irish telephone – as easy as shouting across the North Atlantic – for Courant readers, among them the one in the Executive Residence on Prospect Avenue who couldn't make the trip, his elderly mother.

Watching as he was received by President Eamon DeValera, the famed fighting Irish leader, then 83, at the presidential palace in Dublin's Phoenix Park.

The nearly-blind DeValera talked of Washington Depot, visited as a boy; of a Waterbury watch he once owned that ran rather poorly.

Paying a mid-morning visit with the governor to the home of one of his mother's friends in Ireland, a gnarled woman in her 80s who served us a tumbler of Irish whiskey, warning that if we didn't drink it all, we would suffer the 'curse of Castle Street.' We drank until our eyes seemed to cross.

Standing by the River Suir late in the day, waiting for Dempsey to catch the fish that would be the hoped-for lead for the next day's story read back home in Hartford.

Suddenly a salmon took his lure, between five and six pounds. As two strolling women watched, the fish was netted.

"Ah, the poor thing!" one woman said in a loud voice. "You're going to let it go, aren't you?" All the kings of Munster couldn't have taken that fish from the governor of Connecticut.

Talk warmly of John Dempsey today – governor, public servant. Along with the words that come easiest – gentle, caring, devout, beloved – don't forget him.

"He'd like that."

[The Hartford Courant; Political Insights, by Charles F. J. Morse; June 26, 1989]

Introduction

Dad and JFK

Folks may forever debate the pros and cons of personal memoirs as valuable pieces of history, on the one hand, and self-serving personal aggrandizements, on the other. But, on a very basic, human level, most of us, I would guess, retain some sense of the fundamental capacity to *remember* as a very simple and usual way of keeping something or someone alive. By contrast, most of us have come to know that to *forget* is the next best thing to consigning something or someone to the oblivion of non-existence or death. In some ways, these memoirs were born out of a blatant failure to remember and a concomitant acquiescence to let die. They are the work of an eldest son, whose closeness and loving devotion cannot help but influence the final product.

In July of 1990, Connecticut's Democrats met in a quadrennial convention. In a somewhat casual enumeration of some of the state's former Democratic Governors (Ribicoff, Dempsey, Grasso, O'Neill), Dad was mentioned as if in passing. And yet, this 1990 convention would most likely be the first one in about fifty years that would not count John Noel Dempsey among the attendees. He had died the previous year (July 16, 1989). Heralded by some as among the state's most popular and progressive leaders, touted by others as an unbeatable 'Warhorse' of a campaigner, said to have been a true and effective bipartisan politician and public servant, respected for fairness, openness, and unquestioned honesty, his own party nonetheless failed to remember him, just one year after his sudden death.

The Dempsey Years (1961–1971) were touted as the birthplace of what, today, are considered mainstays of the Connecticut government: The Department of Correction, the Department of Children and Families, The Department of Environmental Protection (established in 1971, months after Dad's retirement), The Department of Community Affairs, The Commission on Higher Education. The courts were improved, new highways were built, the General Fund was created, interest-free loans were made available to college students, and the first appropriations to establish the University of Connecticut Health Center were made, setting the long-sought-after foundation for the state's own medical

14

and dental school. In the obituary for Dad in The New York Times, it was stated: "Former Governor John Dempsey...helped foster Connecticut's reputation in the 1960s as a national trend-setter in social and environmental laws...He served as Connecticut's Governor from 1961–1971, overseeing the passage of a job-training law that became the model for the Federal Manpower Training Act, and the first revision of the Connecticut Constitution in 150 years. In the Dempsey Years, Connecticut was also among the first states to impose restrictions on air and water pollution, well in advance of similar Federal laws." But despite all this, the first anniversary of his untimely death found his own political party, gathered in a statewide convention in Hartford, and for all intents and purposes he and his ten years at the helm were effectively forgotten.

A letter to the Democratic State Central Committee from the members of his family elicited one single response from a member, acknowledging and regretting the omission of any real remembrance on the occasion of the Convention. The deafening silence was an all but unanimous response of the Committee.

So, while it is undeniably true that these memoirs were born of what was originally strong resentment, I hope that they also may testify to an effort to ensure that a failure to remember will NOT mean forgetting either the man or the political period in Connecticut's history, sometimes referred to as The Dempsey Years. My hope is that both the man and his near ten years as Governor of our state will not be neatly consigned to some dusty corner of history, simply because his own party failed to remember him in any significant way. Rather, my hope in writing these memoirs is to ensure preserving for future generations the memory of someone significantly deserving of remembrance.

That hope takes on near imperative proportions, as the cynicism and the distrust and the sense of hopelessness mount whenever words like *politician* or *politics* or even *government* raise their public heads. It's probably fair to say that negativity, if not disdain, modifies most people's perception of public life and the politics thereby engendered. And nothing, absolutely nothing, would have been or could be more hurtful to the man of whose memory I write. If ever there was a man who sincerely believed that public service was a true vocation, it was John Dempsey. And if remembrance can breathe on cooling embers, rekindling them and resurrecting both light and life, then I know of at least one man, never ashamed to refer to himself as a politician, who will be both satisfied and pleased.

When you write something in stone, you expect that it will last and be remembered. But that, of course, presumes that there is someone interested enough to read it. If there is no one to read, then there is no one to remember. On his gravestone, we wrote these words:

John Noel Dempsey
1915 -1989
Governor of Connecticut
Beloved husband, father, grandfather, friend

That is how we saw him, how we knew him, and how we wanted him to be remembered. We placed his title and office of Governor of Connecticut first not because it came first chronologically and not because he cherished it most (that distinction was reserved for the office and title his children gave him!) but because of the great and abiding respect in which he himself held them. But a stone, however lovely it might be, standing in Saint Mary's Cemetery, in Putnam, draws few readers. Perhaps these words, written on paper, will draw a slightly larger readership and so increase the possibility of remembrance.

Without a doubt, it is difficult, if not impossible, for an admiring son to be completely objective about his own father, and I willingly admit to being no exception to that general rule. What I have done is to be perfectly honest and truthful in what I have written, to the best of my abilities and according to the lights that are mine. I make no pretense of being complete in this presentation. On the contrary, I am trying to present those precise aspects of John Dempsey which are not easily or necessarily known to others, or which are at least better known to family than to others. Scores of other people are far better equipped than I am to evaluate his political life and career accomplishments. But few people are better equipped than his own family to share their personal perspectives of the man, whom so many knew as the leader of city and state, but whom they knew, and from up close, as a husband, father, grandfather, and friend.

To the extent that these words help to convey to the reader a better, a fuller picture of the man, they will have succeeded. To the further extent that these words help to dissipate some of the cynicism, now often considered a necessary element in describing the world of politics, they will have enhanced the philosophy by which a man lived his life. And to the furthest extent that these words may, in any small way, encourage and confirm another person to accept political/public life as a personal vocation, then Dad's philosophy that 'politics is people' will truly live. To his memory and to that uncomplicatedly sincere philosophy, these words are dedicated.

Remembering the Beginnings

Dad and his dad, 1933

Edward Patrick Dempsey (Grampy Dempsey) remains a man of some mystery. We believe that he was born in a suburb of Dublin called Rathmines, in or about 1872. To understand the lack of precision, you have to remember that immigrants were often tempted, if not counseled, to understate their actual ages after coming to this country in order to purchase life insurance at a better premium. Apparently, no one ever thought or was overly concerned about the other end of the spectrum, and the additional years one would be expected to work before retirement. We have his birth year listed on immigration documents as both/either 1872 and/or 1873. For some reason, the family opted for 1872. In any case, we know, because he told us, that at a relatively young age, he ran away from home. His own mother had died, and his father had remarried, and contention reigned between this son and his stepmother. He did as so many under-aged lads did in his day, he lied about his actual age and joined the army. A friend of mine presumed and said, "Oh, he joined the Irish army?"

"No," I rejoined. " He enlisted in the British army!"

"An Irishman in the British army?" my friend shouted back, totally forgetting that prior to 1916, Ireland was part of the vast British Empire. Ireland and its people belonged to England's colonial holdings for centuries, and the British army was the only army any Irishman knew. And so, a young Irish runaway, eager to get far from home and to travel and to fight, turned to the one alternative available. And so, Edward Patrick Dempsey, an Irishman, and native of the Dublin area left home and homeland and spent the next twenty-plus years in Her Majesty's military service, defending the British Empire in India and South Africa, as a member of The Queen's Sixteenth Lancers. It was in the army that he learned the tailoring trade; it was there as well that he acquired some of the characteristics that his family counted as his particular habits, if not peculiarities: polishing the family's shoes as if for military parade; making his son's First Communion white outfit; laying out the Sunday morning requisites of a clean handkerchief, rosary, prayer book and collection money, on the kitchen table, three neatly distinct piles, every Saturday night of their family life. Eventually, his military career ground to a halt and he was stationed in a small, cavalry barracks town called Cahir, in south-central Ireland, in County Tipperary. It was there that he 'mustered out,' and it was there that he made the acquaintance of one Ellen Looby, a local and one of the twelve children of a harness-maker, leatherworker, and cobbler, John Looby and his wife Catherine Quigley Looby. [There would ensue, at least on this side of the Atlantic, a running battle as to how to spell the family name correctly. Nana would hold out for 'L dablowbee y,' translated as 'L-double-O-B-Y.' The family name sins would be compounded when the name of Nana's brother John, known as Jack, appeared on the plaque of Putnam's Pomfret Street Bridge, commemorating veterans of World War I. There the family name appeared as 'LUBEY.' Nana's interpretation of all such erroneous spellings was that her siblings were trying to be 'very grand' in this new country. The variant spellings could therefore be easily and correctly dismissed!] Ellen was in her early thirties at the time, and she was working in the houses of some of the town's gentry, specifically the Smiths, owners of the local flour mill, and later for the descendants of the town's Lord Cahir and the Charteris family. Ellen was a servant, often to be found in the kitchen, helping to prepare and serve the family's meals.

County Tipperary seems to have been home to the Looby family for some period of time. The John Loobys had originally married, settled, and had begun raising their family in the town of Cashel. At some point in time, and for some unknown reason, the family had transplanted itself to

Cahir, a smaller town some fifteen miles to the west. There the family continued to grow until it reached what today would be considered substantial proportions. The Loobys were parents to twelve children, and they all lived, presumably compactly, in a house of no more than five smallish rooms (one of which was the leather shop), across from the local blacksmith on Lower Abbey Street, better known locally, even today, as Blind Street. Not all of the children lived to reach adulthood, and by 1913, the surviving Looby children were scattered from England to the United States, with Ellen living at home with her parents.

On February 14, 1914, Edward Patrick Dempsey and Ellen Looby were married at Cahir's local parish church, Saint Mary's, and then it was back to Blind Street, where the newlyweds took up residence with the remaining Loobys. And it was there, on January 3, 1915, that John Noel Dempsey was born. He was named for his maternal grandfather, and the middle name, Noel, was given since he had been born during the twelve days of Christmas. According to the church records, he was baptized two days after his birth, on January 5, 1915. Friends of his parents, Edward O'Dwyer and Katherine Griffin stood as godparents. And as if to confirm the persistence of coincidence, the officiating priest was listed as Father R. Meskel. In 1971, as Dad left the Governor's office, he would be succeeded by Thomas J. Meskill.

In 1965, as Mom and Dad and I visited a parish church in Cashel, a woman came over to us. "You're Governor Dempsey, aren't you?", she said. "How well I remember the day you were born! I was a friend of your mother's, and I remember bicycling from Cashel to Cahir when the news came that Nell Looby had had her baby." She bore no distinctly unusual news about her visit to Cahir that January day, but her remembering my father's birth brought great delight and a sense of warm gratitude for her remembering and for this unexpected connection with the past.

Neither Grampy Dempsey nor Nana Dempsey (Ned and Nell to one another), was what you'd call 'a kid' at the time of Dad's birth. Grampy was about forty-two, and Nana was about thirty-five when their son and only child was born. To our knowledge, Grampy himself had been an only child too (or at least the only one he knew of); Nana was one of twelve Looby children, but Dad was the only second-generation representative of either side of the two families known to have survived childhood and attained adulthood. Two male children had been born to Nana's sister, Julia Looby, and her husband in the States, but both boys died in infancy or early childhood. Like his father, Dad was destined to be an only child, and a child without any cousins or other relatives approximating his age. He was born to older parents, and he would be raised knowing only elders as family. He seems to have been treated as a 'young adult' from his earliest days, and his father's expectations would seem to have been those for a mature, well-disciplined young man. I often wonder how much genuine childhood Dad got to enjoy. His father 'ruled the roost,' and he seemed never content with 'second-best.' Some of that passed on to Dad, who could on occasion be heard to reflect over a recent report card: "Now, with a little more effort, I'll bet that A– could have been an A...or even an A+." No one, it seems, is exempt from a certain brush with perfectionism! Things like 'duty' and 'responsibility' were deemed necessary virtues, touted frequently and heartily.

Dad's status as an only child (of an only-child father to boot) has, over the years, given rise to some amusing situations or stories. On a visit to Alabama, a maternal cousin came back from a visit to a local chiropractor, and she brought with her the doctor's business card engraved Dr…Dempsey, DC. When my cousin had shared that we were visiting from Connecticut and that we too were Dempseys, the doctor smiled as if knowingly and assured her that he and she were cousins then, too, because 'Governor Dempsey was my cousin; his father and my father were brothers.' Pat came home embarrassed to ask, "I thought Uncle John's dad was an only child, wasn't he? Then how is the Chiropractor his cousin?" It's one of those things that only the Irish can understand! Or another time, a man assured my brother that he knew Dad's brother and remembered Dad so very well; after all, they had all gone to high school together. When pressed to name the high school, he named some school in Hartford. Dad never left Putnam till 1961, long, long after his high school years. Today, I guess, these would simply be dubbed 'alternative facts' and stacked on the growing mound of such.

In Cahir, Grampy's workstation seems to have been at the very top of the flour mill, where he worked, with ample windows affording an unobstructed view of Castle Street, the mall, the River Suir, and its weir. When Dad was in elementary school, at the Sisters of Mercy convent, his mother worked in the kitchen of Cahir House, on the Square, around the corner from the school. Cahir House today and since 1928, is a well-established hotel. But earlier, this rather magnificent building was the home of the descendants of the Lords of Cahir, a British family who quite literally had owned the town and everything in it. So, like proverbial bookends, Grampy in the mill and Nana at Cahir House, his parents could and did keep a fairly close watch on the comings and goings of the locals, their son among them. From Dad's memories of those early days, it seems as though his parents had succeeded in convincing him of their omnipresence. One day as he and several of his friends sauntered home after school, they probably dawdled on their way, maybe hanging on the bridge, eyes on the water flowing swiftly over the weir, wondering what fish there might be lurking, when the quiet of the afternoon was rent by an ear-splitting whistle from the top of the mill. There followed a bellow and a crooked finger: "You! Home! No slinging!" The youngster's worst fears had been confirmed: His father DID see and know everything!

Though far removed from the larger urban centers of the country, Cahir was not spared the effects of the turbulent years of the Irish Rebellion, between 1916 and 1920. Firstly, there had been the Easter Uprising of 1916 and then the ensuing war seeking independence from England. Every Irish family has its own memories and stories of these days, and the Dempseys were no exception. It is said by some that Grampy used his experience and training as a British soldier to help train and drill some of the Cahir 'locals,' who fought for their country's freedom. One of Dad's earliest memories, stemming from these years, was that of an afternoon when he and a group of other Cahir youngsters were rounded up on their way home from school and held at the far end of the mall, probably by some Black-and-Tans

(English mercenaries with mismatched uniforms) presumably as potential hostages. After some anxious hours, all of the children were released to their worried and angry parents. I often wonder at whose hands these miscreants of hostage-takers would have fared worse, Grampy's or Nana's. To take a child as a possible hostage was really scratching the bottom of the proverbial barrel, even for the Black-and-Tans. For these no-longer-young parents, I can't imagine a greater or more embittering threat to their notion of parenthood as guardians and protectors of their only son.

Independence from England, realized by a cease-fire or truce on July 11, 1921, after six years of rebellion and warfare, brought no utopia to a war- and poverty-ravaged Ireland. Instead, a bloody civil war ensued. And not unlike civil wars the world over, this one left traces of division, discontent, and bitterness down through the years, achieving what centuries of English occupation had never been able to do – divide the Irish among themselves. With the tyrannical treatment of the occupying English, the Irish, who had been dispossessed of almost everything, had a common enemy and a united cause: To fight against injustice and bigotry. But a civil war – a war in which factions divide and support opposing sides of a question – a civil war was a completely different entity. Reminiscent of the New Testament prediction of a division of father from son, a mother from daughter, the Irish people took sides over the question of the composition of the newly independent country: Would the six northern counties (what is now Northern Ireland) be part of the newly formed Republic, or not? Six of the nine northern counties, the

Province of Ulster, had been and remained a bastion of English political, military, economic, and social power and influence. These counties were overwhelmingly Protestant and showed no interest in being joined (or rejoined) to the south of the country. Nothing, in hundreds of years, had affected the people of this tiny nation so viscerally and so divisively, and nothing would leave longer or deeper traces of unforgiving remembrance. Two portions of the Cashel Looby family were typical. The Caseys (who were Loobys) and the Quigleys pledged opposing allegiances, and, apparently, neither family had spoken to the other since the early 1920s. This unrelenting and deafening silence was something that Dad would never really understand or accept. It was clearly visible in his face, in 1965, whenever 'the Troubles' were raised in actuality or in conversation. In his experience and belief system, people could disagree, even strongly and vociferously, but they could never afford to allow differences to divide them from one another. Grudges, whatever their bases, in fact, were simply not part of his repertory. Even on the occasion of my ordination to the diaconate in Cahir, August of 1966, both the Looby/Caseys and the Quigleys were invited, and they attended. But their carefully maintained separation from one another that day was, depending on the point of view, either painfully hurtful or childishly ludicrous. But what was indisputable was that the enmity was real and ongoing, even more than forty years after the original disagreement. And as Dad was heard to say: "It's just sad, so sad!"

By 1924, when Dad was then nine years old, Grampy and Nana had come to a decision: Their future, especially that of their young son, seemed the brightest in the United

States. By this time, Blind Street was devoid of Loobys, and just the three Dempseys remained across from the forge; no local family ties remained; in fact, all other remaining Loobys were either in England or in the United States. Years later, Grampy would say that the dual goals of education and employment for their son were the convincing considerations. Ireland had survived both a war of independence and civil war, and Ireland by 1925 was paying the price for both. The future seemed westward, and so the decision was made to emigrate. In late summer 1925, all plans were set and all farewells were said. The three Dempseys left Cahir and headed for Cobh or Queenstown, ready to board a Boston-bound liner. But then, a ship's medical officer, after a cursory physical examination, determined that Grampy had a heart condition severe enough to prohibit emigration to America. However, for a certain specified financial consideration, the cardiac condition could be miraculously cured, and the trio could proceed on their way. My imagining is that to say my grandfather was angry would be the mildest understatement; apoplectic might be more like it. The very idea of a kickback was repugnant, and the accusation of a heart defect was an intolerable blow to his male pride. Bag and baggage in hand, the three returned to Cahir, discouraged but determined. After some weeks of 'discussions' with White Star Line officials and emigration folks, it was determined that 'an error' had doubtlessly been made. They returned to Cobh and set sail without further incident.

Census records indicate that the Dempsey Three arrived in Boston aboard the Celtic on August 30, 1925. With the

Atlantic crossed and a safe and uneventful arrival achieved, they headed for Putnam, Connecticut, where Nana's family had earlier settled.

By dint of his twenty-plus years in the British Army, Grampy had done some traveling as a soldier, specifically to India and to South Africa, so one may suppose some familiarity if not necessarily comfortability with traveling. And Nana herself had crossed the Atlantic once before. In 1907, she had chaperoned her youngest sibling, Jack Looby, when he immigrated to the States. In later years, she would recall that during the winter months, she had never been so cold in all her life! In 1908, when a letter arrived saying that their mother was ill back in Cahir, she eagerly grasped the opportunity and returned to Tipperary.

I can't help but sometimes wonder if there was anyone dockside to greet them, or did they have to struggle with the vast newness and, like true pioneers, scramble to find their way to a new and different destination. Whatever their initial fate, the three of them somehow arrived at 303 South Main Street, Putnam, the established home of the American Loobys: Julia Looby and her husband, Jeremiah Maher, Catherine Looby, Jim Looby, and, at least on occasion, Mary Looby, and Jack Looby, the youngest of the Cahir clan. These were Nana's siblings and, I would suppose, the legal sponsors of the newly arrived immigrants. The house was large (certainly by Irish standards and in comparison with the tiny house on Blind Street), eight rooms in two stories, set on three-quarters of an acre of land, much of which Jim had turned into a vegetable garden. To the right and rear of the property lived Mary Denning, another Irish immigrant, whose sister and brother-in-law, Tom and

Deborah (Lynch) Toolan, would become two of the first and best friends the new arrivals would ever know. Across South Main Street lived the Bradfords, a family who traced their roots to the Mayflower, and whose close friendship was cherished till the last of them disappeared. Differences, whether of age, religion, ethnicity, race, or politics seemed to matter little most of the time, and that acceptance of and appreciation for diversity would mark my father all of his earthly days.

Once again, the young John Dempsey would find himself surrounded by older people, at home at least, if not at school. But school too would underline the difference. Years later, one of his schoolmates, Loretta St. Onge Johnston, would tell me that she distinctly remembered Dad's first day at Israel Putnam Elementary School. "I knew about your Dad even before I ever met him," she said. "Word had gone around the schoolyard at recess that there was a new kid in school, and he talked funny!" Dad remembered comments about his accent, his clothing, and even his education. Teachers were perplexed and uncertain about the grade in which to place the foreigner. After several days in one grade, his performance seemed to convince them of his ability to cope with the rigors of the next highest grade, and so he was 'promoted.' Once the inevitable newness had worn off, he adapted to his school setting and became almost indistinguishable from the rest of the students, except, perhaps, for the distinct lilt of his occasional words, a trace of which was never far from him, even in adulthood.

Ireland's climate would have to be said to be moderate. Below zero temperatures were rare; snowfall was only occasional, light, and short-lived. Roses continued to bloom in front gardens even up to Christmas. And although the winter days were darkly gloomy and humid if not downright wet, spring and summer days could be long and sunny and mild. Extremes of either heat or cold were exceptional. The climate of the new country, however, was vastly different, especially in the severity of its coldness, and for a ten-year-old, who had arrived clad in short pants and knee-socks, the change was drastic.

Life at home could not have been terribly exciting for a ten-year-old boy. The highlight of the week, he would later confide, was the Sunday afternoon appearance of a well-worn Victrola, accompanied by its complement of even more worn records. The schedule varied seldom: Morning Mass, Sunday dinner, followed by recorded entertainment! There was an ancient gramophone and about a half dozen records. For a ten-year-old, the recorded thrill soon passed, and even the somewhat strained school ambiance must have seemed preferable.

It could not have been with great sadness that in the first half of 1926, once again thanks to Tom Toolan, the new immigrants left South Main Street and moved into their own place, a mill house on Putnam's High Street, somewhat dubiously dubbed 'Pigeon Hill.' It would be several years more before the duplex at 15 Church Street became available, and there they settled and lived, again in mill housing, my father until his marriage in 1940, my grandfather until his death in 1951, and my grandmother until her move to the Governor's Residence in 1961. My grandparents were probably quite happy with their new 'digs.' 15 Church Street was not at all unlike Blind Street in

Cahir, a mere spit from a river, in sight of the mill, a rented space, two rooms down and two rooms up, and with the privy 'at the bottom of the garden,' on the banks of the Quinebaug River. They had come a long way only to find a facsimile of what they had left behind.

From all remembered reports and retold stories, Dad's years at Putnam High School were full and happy and productive ones. Of course, there were the traumas of trying to get an Irish tongue around French syllables (a task which Mr. Dupre approached undaunted) and the not uncommon problems of balancing a major in sports with a minor in academics. But, all in all, he both enjoyed tremendously and profited considerably from his high school years. French aside, his major preoccupations were with football, basketball, track, and baseball. Some would have us believe that preoccupations of a somewhat romantic nature also pulled him in certain less academic directions, but he always downplayed such rumors and sought refuge in forced testimony from my mother. He was a senior, and she was a freshman, but…that's another story for later, maybe!

The halcyon days of high school ended with graduation in June of 1934. His academic prowess (an achievement which he never tired of touting, as remonstration against any rumors to the contrary) gained him acceptance into Providence College in neighboring Rhode Island. To these hallowed halls, he and a group of fellow stalwarts commuted each day, sharing a car and the 'freight' of the daily trip. Just as his first college year was ending in 1935, his father became ill, and family necessity forced his entry into the Putnam Woolen Mill. He never returned to Providence College, though that one year of university-level study marked him for life. He retained a high level of regard for the Dominican Friars, who taught him; he loved the dialectics of debate; he respected the desire for pursuing formal education beyond high school, even if it could not be his. In later life, two events would serve to crystallize his fondness for his alma mater. In 1963, his godson, John J. Kelly, Jr., was a member of the Providence College graduating class. Dad was asked to be the commencement speaker, and the college conferred on him an honorary doctoral degree. He was delighted, to say the least. In his mind, it seemed as if the impossibility of the 1930s was corrected or at least amended, and what he had learned over the past nearly thirty years was given credence and formal affirmation. In 1969, my brother, Kevin, graduated from Providence College, and thereby gave Dad one of his finest and proudest moments. His son had now accomplished what he had not been able to do, and events had come full circle. His parents' decision to emigrate in search of fuller educational opportunities for their son, combined with his own forced withdrawal from college, effectively wrought a consistent and outspoken advocate for higher education. In later life, he would be delighted to have the power to increase the state's capacity to offer higher education to more of its citizens. The development and growth of the state's community college system was a near dream come true for him. I have to believe that he continued to see and respect other students, not like himself at a younger age, struggling with family responsibilities and yet yearning for a college education. What had been impossible for him could be possible for them; his dream could become theirs; and what he could not have, he could somehow facilitate the state's offering to others. One of the reasons for emigrating would find delightful fulfillment in the accomplishments of others. And few things could have made him a happier man!

Remembering Home

Mom and Dad with the Irish President, 1965

How many times in the mid-nineteen fifties, during my high school years, I was asked: "Where are you from?"

'Putnam' was my inevitable response, and just as inevitably came the usual query: "Is that in Connecticut?"

Northeastern Connecticut, the so-called Quiet Corner, indeed the whole of Eastern Connecticut, has often been regarded and dubbed the state's Appalachia. Few of my seminary classmates had ever heard of Putnam, nor, apparently, had many of my teachers. The seminary rector, who had the commission of delivering monthly spiritual lectures to the Daughters of the Holy Spirit in Putnam, delighted in regaling the assembled seminarians with tales of his recent trip out to 'Poot-nam,' with no intention, I am sure, of yanking my chain! Undoubtedly because of the draw of an established family, my father and his parents had chosen to settle in Putnam, whose principal industry was the manufacture of textiles: Thread and silk and wool. From 1925, Putnam would be home, and it would remain so, for some of us, for the rest of our lives, regardless of where we might be living at any given time. Despite his insistence with each of his children that we exercise responsibility and adult maturity in matters pertaining to prior planning, Dad never said or did anything about where he would eventually want to be buried. And yet, they had lived in Putnam, then Hartford, then Groton over a period of almost thirty years. At the end of a dinnertime discussion, I raised the previously unspoken question with him directly. "Now, where do you think I'd want to be buried? What kind of question is that? At home, of course!" No one doubted what he meant by 'home.' In the early eighties, with nothing pressing or particular in mind, I purchased a four-plot lot, at home, in Saint Mary's Cemetery. At the time of the purchase, I knew nothing specific about the lot, except that it was in the same section of the cemetery as the graves of my Dempsey grandparents and great-aunt, Kate. Like so many things that seemed unimportant at the time, I filed the deed away for future use, far distant future use, and asked for no further details. In July of 1989, the day before his funeral and burial, Mom asked if we could swing by the cemetery to see where we would be going the next day. It was easy enough to find the newly dug grave in the old section. It was only then that we noticed that his grave would be in a direct line with, three lots removed from, that of his parents. That line of monuments would now reveal the name DEMPSEY twice. "Home is where the heart is," it is said. Or perhaps, home is where the heart lies buried.

Sometime in the mid-1930s, or so the story goes, Church Street neighbors had a concern about a street light. Someone would have to go to the City Fathers and plead their cause. The lot fell to a twenty-year-old, known for his articulate presentations and his powers of persuasion. Whatever the original concern had been, the neighbors were apparently pleased with their young representative's efforts on their behalf, and when, in April of 1937, the Democratic Party was looking for a person to succeed the deceased Alderman, Edward Duffy, they chose John Dempsey, recently admitted as an elector of the city of Putnam the previous September. It would seem that the rest of the ward's voters must have agreed with his neighbors because he was elected to his first public office, that of Alderman, representing his neighborhood, Ward 4, in December of 1937. That election brought an entirely new slate of Democrats into office. Harry C. Kelly was elected mayor, and 'for the first time in twenty-two years, in a city election, Putnam Democrats on Monday swept their entire ticket into office on a surprise tidal wave that carried everything before it.' (The Windham County Observer; December 8, 1937)

From age twenty-two, and for the next thirty-four years of his public life and for an additional eighteen years thereafter, John Dempsey's staunchly proud affiliation with the Democratic Party would lead him to his state's highest elected office and to a place of deep respect in the minds and hearts of those original Putnam electors. His career was launched, but its flight would not be without turbulence – as if any ever is! And through it all, Putnam would become better-known (if not well-known), and the quiet mill town would remain 'home.' From Putnam, he waged numerous campaigns for other public offices. In Putnam, he continued to live until the day he formally assumed the office of Governor on January 24, 1961. To Putnam, he returned to 'wind up' campaigns and to celebrate the joys of approaching retirement from public office, until he returned, a final time, on July 19, 1989. Like the Gospel parable's mustard seed, and like the tiny acorn of Connecticut's mighty Charter Oak, the smallness of the beginning was totally disproportionate to the ending.

In December of 1938, just about a year after the stunning Democratic victory, Mayor Kelly resigned. His successor was not a Democrat but a wildly popular Republican, William McCoy, a man for whom Dad had the greatest respect, admiration, and genuine fondness.

The elections of 1939 saw the Democrats field candidates led by Perry Barber, for Mayor, and John Dempsey, for Alderman-at-Large. Dad had succeeded Perry Barber as chairman of the Putnam Democratic Town Committee in October 1939, and now he faced his first city-wide race – no longer within the relative safety of Ward 4, but exposed to the electorate of the entire city. The Democrats prevailed, and Perry Barber became the third Democratic mayor in twenty-four years. On January 3, 1940, the new mayor appointed Dad to the salaried position of Clerk of the Water Department. That day was Dad's twenty-fifth birthday, and what a gift! After working in the

Putnam Woolen Mill, from the time he had left Providence College in 1935 until this January day in 1940, Dad would now have 'an office job,' with a salary of twenty-six dollars a week. How could things have worked out better for a young man about to be married to his high school sweetheart in July of that same year? The 'land of opportunity' was, indeed, true to its name, and the country of his adoption was a genuine mother to this newly-adopted son.

An interesting yet often overlooked happening in that city election of 1939 was the election of yet another Dempsey. Dad's father, Edward Patrick Dempsey, had been chosen to replace his son as the candidate for Alderman from Ward 4. Along with the rest of the Democratic ticket, he too was carried on that tidal wave of success, and he would serve as Alderman for the next two-year term. Now, without telling tales outside the confines of the family, it certainly would be fair to say that the presence of two Dempseys on the same Aldermanic Council must have made for some interesting and highly vocal moments. For whatever reasons of human psychodynamics, Dad and his father had a distinct proclivity for disagreeing with one another...regarding just about everything! Both loved baseball, and both rooted for Boston: Dad for the Red Sox and Grampy for the Braves! Both loved a game of cards (usually Pitch/Set-Back), but seldom did their strategies for victory agree! My own sense is that if Dad said 'black,' Grampy would say 'white,' and if Grampy said 'up,' then Dad would say 'down!' I often wondered if it was a case of two people being so diametrically different, or if, in fact, it was that they were so very much alike! Whatever the case may have been, it's almost impossible for me to imagine these two stalwart Democrats, simultaneous members of the Common Council, agreeing with one another on just about anything. IF they did, then it was almost certainly the only arena in which they ever consistently agreed with one another. [The impossibility of any harmonious co-existence is borne out in the rumored decision of the Town Committee that only one Dempsey should run for a seat on the Council the next time around! A prohibition not enforced for several years.]

Perhaps the single most obvious casualty of this father-son situation was my grandmother. A self-styled peacemaker, she would often find herself embroiled in one of their discussions (not to say arguments!) at home. I can still remember times when the peacemaker would try to ply her skills by saying: "You're right, John," and in the very next breath saying, "You're right, Ned!" Unfortunately, her sole success lay in diverting their focused attention, momentarily, from the issue at hand to HER! The attempt at peace usually merited little more than warnings, from one or the other or both, to 'stay out of it,' something she never seemed able to do for very long.

In the city's elections of 1941, the Democrats again swept to victory, days before the horrors of Pearl Harbor. Dad and Grampy returned to the Council as Alderman-at-large and Alderman from Ward 4 once again, and the Dempseys, doubtless, continued to disagree!

The elections of December 1943 witnessed changes. The Republican candidate, Harvey Grinsell, Sr., defeated Perry Barber for the office of Mayor. Dad, however, was re-elected to the post of Alderman-at-large; Grampy (to the relief, I would guess, of the rest of the Council) had not run for re-election. There began one of those politically-sensitive periods in which neither party has total control of the entire situation. I've sometimes wondered if these two years were Dad's novitiate in the school of compromise and negotiation, skills that would become essentials in the years ahead.

In the Fall of 1945, Dad became the Democratic nominee for the office of Mayor. His opponent would be the incumbent Mayor, whose popularity would carry the day. For the first time since his entry into the political scene, Dad was defeated at the polls, and the upstart would be made to pay the price for insurrection. As if to underline the seriousness of this situation, and, probably, to make an incontrovertible point, one of the first orders of business in January 1946 was to reassess and realign mayoral appointments within the city's government. Dad held two paid positions: One as a part-time Secretary to the Board of Police Commissioners, and the other was the full-time position as Clerk of the Water Department. On January 18, 1946, he had neither position! The Windham County Observer, not a particularly pro-Democratic newspaper, wrote: "Outstanding in the exemplification of partisan and steam-roller politics was the ousting of John Dempsey." For the first time since 1935, Dad was without a job. But the situation was a bit more serious now; he had a wife and a four-and-a-half-year-old son, with another baby about to be born on January 24th. It could not have been comfortable, to put it mildly. But there was greater discomfort as well. At least one of the members of the Board of Police Commissioners, a man considered a friend, had concurred in Dad's firing. That seemed to hurt more than the electoral defeat, more even than the prospect of being jobless. It hurt because it seemed a personal betrayal, a breach of friendship, a loss of trust.

[Never the diplomat that Dad would become, my mother recalls entering the A&P on January 19th, manifestly pregnant, and, raised to her full five feet one inch height, and telling the erstwhile friend exactly what she thought of him and precisely where he could go! Rarely has anyone seen Mom enraged, and even just hearing about it, years after the fact, makes me wish that I could remember having been there. It was, in its own way, a kind of history-in-the-making.]

The Putnam Patriot of January 17, 1946, went on to comment about the Republican administration's decision: "…by a Three-Two vote of the G.O.P.-controlled Police Commission, Dempsey was victimized by admitted application of the Spoils System as far as the secretarial berth of that group is concerned, and in direct contrast to the existing Merit System under which the Board is governed."

But victory was to be snatched from the jaws of defeat by a telephone conversation that January. The caller commiserated over the recent losses of election and jobs, and the caller asked if the two of them might meet in the near future. That meeting and its continuing aftermath would affect Dad's career forever after. The caller was none other than eastern Connecticut's elected representative to the United States Congress's House of Representatives, a woman, hailing from Scotland, CT, a woman by the name of Chase Going Woodhouse. In addition to the offer of sympathy, she offered a job. The first week of February

1946 found Dad as the Congresswoman's Field Secretary, her representative 'at home' in eastern Connecticut. For the remaining months of this, her first term in the seventy-ninth Congress, Dad would become a federal employee and travel the length and breadth of the Second Congressional District, learning other facets of public life and its political realities, meeting both constituents and pundits, broadening his scope and visibility, becoming increasingly enamored of the highly energetic and keenly intelligent woman who was his 'boss' and teacher. Though their time together as working colleagues was relatively short, their relationship would outlast both of their public careers and would deepen in mutual respect and abiding trust. Dad was never known to be a very 'formal' person, and yet, in his dealings with Chase Going Woodhouse, I never heard him refer to her as anything other than 'Ma'am.' From that time forward, he was both proud and truthful in acknowledging that Chase Going Woodhouse was his 'mentor.' And I can't think of a finer tribute to a courageous lady from a proud and grateful protégé.

Undaunted by the defeat of 1945, Dad was nominated and elected Alderman-at-large in the Democratic sweep of December 1947. In 1948, he was nominated, for the first of three times, for the office of State Representative. In all three elections, he was successful, and his success was further crowned with the companionship of a kind and gentle fellow Representative, Norman LaRose, a fellow Democrat, an equally staunch advocate for Putnam and eastern Connecticut, a friend.

In August of 1949, the Democratic Mayor of Putnam, Perry Barber, was named a Judge, and the Alderman-at-large assumed the mayoralty. In December of that same year, Dad was elected Mayor, an office in which he would proudly and continuously serve until January 9, 1961, days before assuming the Governorship of the state. But electoral disappointment had yet one further hand to deal him.

In 1954, the state Democratic Party nominated him as their candidate for the office of Lieutenant Governor. He forwent the local nomination for State Representative and plunged into his first statewide political campaign. It was to be a year of electoral dichotomies. The entire Democratic ticket, with the notable exception of Abraham Ribicoff, was resoundingly defeated; the entire Republican ticket, with the equally notable exception of the incumbent Governor, John Lodge, was triumphant. For the second time in his public career, Dad would taste the bitter dregs, yet out of them, he would claim nectar. In January 1955, Governor Ribicoff took the oath of office; he would have by his side not an elected cabinet of Democratic state officials but the unsuccessful candidate for the Lieutenant Governorship, his new Executive Aide (or as the Governor sometimes put it: "My eyes and ears outside the door"). For the next four years, through floods, political skirmishes, and legislative wars, Dad would come to know the intricacies of state government from a priceless vantage point. The future years were being shaped and formed and founded in ways unknown to anyone, even the most astute political observer.

These statewide elections of 1954 would become history in at least one significant way. They, I believe, would mark the last time that candidates for Governor and Lieutenant Governor would run separately, rather than as a team or entity. Future days would not again see a

Democratic governor with a Republican Lieutenant Governor, or vice versa, and no longer would an Executive Aide need to become the Governor's unofficial lieutenant.

The quadrennial cycle returned the Democrats to a search for candidates for the 1958 elections. In late spring or early summer of that year, Mom and Dad began a lengthy series of discussions, to which we, as children, were privy, but only in snippets. It seems that 'The Party' was again looking to grace Dad with the nomination for the Lieutenant Governorship, as they had in 1954. But things were different now, at least in Mom's eyes. For the past four years, Dad's annual salary for the position of Executive Aide had been fifteen thousand dollars, a not insignificant or inconsiderable amount, given the times and the geographical location of the home. It would have been difficult to imagine earning that amount in many other ways. Sure, it meant a two-way commute to Hartford and home, but locally a fifteen thousand dollar a year salary would have been otherwise hard to come by. However, the Party's tendered opportunity carried with it an annual salary of a mere five thousand dollars (one-third of his current earnings!) AND a car! While Dad valiantly touted the 'opportunity,' 'the car,' and loyalty to The Party, Mom remained unmoved in her logic that she could not 'cook a car,' or 'clothe the kids' with opportunity, or 'pay the bills' with loyalty! But the strength of logic met its match, and, in what later came to be known as 'the usual compromise,' Mom relented and accepted that reasonableness is not the sole criterion for decisions. She would later explain, in a way uniquely hers: "What good would the money have been if Dad were unhappy?" Dad was duly nominated, and in

45

January 1959, became Lieutenant Governor, where he would preside over the workings of the Senate. And the Dempsey's Putnam driveway now sported a shiny new black Cadillac, complete with license plates, proclaiming: 'Official 2.'

On January 21, 1961, Governor Ribicoff resigned the governorship to become Secretary of Health, Education, and Welfare in the Camelot cabinet of the recently elected President John Fitzgerald Kennedy. In accordance with the tenets of the Connecticut Constitution, Dad assumed the office of governor on his predecessor's resignation. In a simple ceremony in the Hall of the House of Representatives, he would publicly take the oath of office on January 24th (my brother John's fifteenth birthday), and that night would find him 'going home' to a place other than Putnam for the first time since his arrival in this country, more than thirty-five years earlier. On the previous Sunday, the people of Putnam had turned out in considerable numbers to say goodbye. By now, he was truly one of their own, and, as his good friend, Cam Tetreault, had said, although they were proud of his accomplishments and happy for his good fortune, they would miss him, their mayor and neighbor and friend. He knew so many of them by name and anecdote, and they had come to trust him with almost anything. The parting, indeed, would be 'sweet sorrow,' and nobody could see the morrow. Their gratitude to him was second only to his gratitude to them; they had been his home.

I remain aware of only those two occasions on which Dad ran for public office and lost the election: Once for Mayor of Putnam, the other for Lieutenant Governor of

Connecticut. To say that these electoral losses didn't hurt, or that they didn't leave certain traces would be to lie. But it would be equally untrue to surmise that they were totally negative experiences; clearly, they were not! In Dad's characteristic fashion, he managed to snatch elusive victory from the jaws of obvious defeat. Very simply, he would wax philosophical and invite us to speculate with him: If he hadn't been defeated in the race for mayor, he might never have gone to work for Chase Going Woodhouse, and without her as guide and mentor, would he ever have made politics his life? And if he hadn't been defeated in the contest for the lieutenant governorship, would he ever have had the chance of being Executive Aide (to Governor Ribicoff)? And what better apprenticeship was there for what would become his future? And had he not run again for Lieutenant Governor (and won, this time!), he never would have been the legal inheritor of that office, which he would hold for ten years, an office and position which he quite literally cherished, respected, and honored all the days of his life! Nothing was ever totally negative; there was always some good to be derived, to be learned, to be discovered. All you had to do was to look and to see things with eyes that searched for goodness everywhere. And hadn't his faith taught him that 'God is good!' It all seemed quite simple and quite sensible to him. What a glorious legacy for anyone willing to accept it!

No retelling of the stories of home would be complete without unraveling the story of the governor and two friends.

More than likely, it was first in late high school or in the years immediately following graduation, that Dad met John

Kelly. Each man would go on to serve as the other's Best Man at their weddings and godfather for each man's firstborn. To say that they were different from one another is to downplay the reality. Uncle Jack could be as precipitous as Dad could be cautious, as fast to 'fly off the handle' as Dad was to be measured, as bellicose as Dad could be pacific. And yet, their friendship weathered years and distances, agreements and disagreements, similarities and differences. But through it all, ups and downs, theirs was a friendship that lasted and deepened with time, and the two families became conjoint: uncles, aunts cousins. And as the Dempseys were a very small tribe, the addition of the Kellys was and is one of life's most appreciated blessings.

In the mid-1940s, while Mom and Dad and I were still living in the apartment on Bradley Street in Putnam, we made the acquaintance of Marilyn Lowry, a friend of our landlords' and, perhaps, a sometime babysitter for me, the toddler. Marilyn was known as 'Sister' or 'Sis,' a name given to her by her brothers, who perhaps struggled with pronouncing 'Marilyn.' Some few years later, now happily married to Roland Bonosconi, Marilyn and Roland came to live on our street, South Main Street. The friendship was renewed and would continue to grow over the years. Marilyn would sometimes be mistaken for my mother's biological sister (most likely because Mom often referred to Marilyn as 'Sis'). And Roland, the plumber, would become Dad's 'fishing buddy' and his nightly confidant in summer, as they sat in the tin rowboat, awaiting the elusive fish of Alexander's Lake. Years later, Roland would go to work at the state's Department of Consumer Protection, for one of its boards of occupational licensing. If the department was going to license plumbers, who better as a director than an actual plumber? Dad may have known nothing about plumbing, but once again he had the good sense to find someone who did know and to put that person in charge.

I know from overhearing comments made by folks in sophisticated Hartford that the how's and why's and wherefore's of these relationships eluded them.

"Who are these guys?"

"What's the connection?"

I guess some folks just couldn't recognize and understand the simplicity and richness of genuine friendship. And that is precisely what Dad had and enjoyed and appreciated with Uncle Jack and with Roland – they were his friends…always!

In the English language, we have lots of sayings, all of which, in one way or another, affirm and confirm the very same truth:

"What goes around, comes around."

"What goes up must come down."

"Earth to earth, ashes to ashes, dust to dust." For Dad it was always crystal clear: "At home, of course! I want to be buried at home." His life unalterably points in one consistent direction: To the northeast, to Putnam, to home. 'You can't go home again' certainly contains its share of truth, but not all truth. 'Look homeward, angel' probably says as much, and with a lot more hope. For, when all is said and done, 'home is where the heart is.'

Remembering A Father

The Dempsey Clan inauguration, 1967

My memories of him drift back to the forties when we lived in an apartment on Bradley Street in Putnam. In my mind, I picture a tall, slim man with swept-back black hair and a handsome face. It's most probably because of my size at age three or four that I remember him as being 'tall,' though many others, over the years, characterized him in much the same way. And yet, he was never 'tall' by any modern standards, at five feet ten inches. The slimness probably helped to project an image taller than its reality. In any case, tall or not so tall, I recall an avid fisherman, who with Irving Miron, our neighbor and landlord from downstairs, swapped tales, secrets, and lures in the basement. It was there that I first encountered a fishing net, with its long handle and mesh pouch. Totally oblivious to its original and real purpose, I picked it up and began 'passing the basket,' just as they did each Sunday in church. I don't remember either fisherman as being a particularly generous contributor to my collection, but Dad said that I had the right idea. Since coins obviously would fall through the mesh, he felt that I must have been looking for 'a silent collection,' i.e. of bills only. Later in life, Dad jokingly referred to this as the beginning of a priestly vocation.

We went fishing together a couple of times that I recall, though I can't imagine that he ever got much real fishing done with me tagging along. Certainly most memorable was the afternoon we spent fishing the Five Mile River in Putnam. Dad landed a fish to be proud of, and he entrusted the prize to me; I was to put it in the nearby creel. I evidently had other ideas, and I found a 'nice safe place' for the fish, covering it lovingly with leaves on the ground, and never seeing that fish again. Search as we did, there was no sign or trace of the beleaguered trout. The event gave deeper meaning to the perennial excuse of 'the one that got away.' Through the years of retelling, the story probably became somewhat embellished and the trout somewhat larger, as that kind of story tends to do, but never was there anything other than good-natured humor and kidding about the one fish that truly got away. To this day, it's hard for me to put anything away for 'safe keeping' without embarrassed smiles at the thought of that safe but missing fish. I never did become a fisherman, but it certainly wasn't for Dad's lack of understanding and trying.

In the winter of 1945, my great uncle, Jim Looby, died, and his sister, Kate, the last of the Loobys on South Main Street, decided to give up the house, about a mile from downtown, and to move in with my grandparents. When Nana asked her sister what she intended to do with the house, Kate, apparently somewhat flummoxed, said: "Well, sure, there's only John and Mary!" And so she did the most obvious logical thing to do: She gave the house and property to my parents. 303 South Main Street would thus become our home for the next sixteen years, until the very day on which the family moved into Hartford's Executive Residence. As World War II drew to a close, the apartment dwellers began the lengthy and arduous process of 'getting the house in shape' for our eventual move. But post-World War II evidenced a housing shortage, and a young couple with a toddler could hardly have even imagined themselves as being homeowners, and yet such they were, with no mortgage to boot. Yet, lest I paint too rosy a picture, the house was hardly move-in ready. The house lacked central heating, and it boasted, not a bathroom, but a single toilet in a closet under the stairway leading to the second floor. The kitchen had running water but only cold water, from a single spigot in an immense cast iron kitchen sink. My father's return to the home which had first welcomed him and his parents in 1925 must have brought back some of his earliest memories of life in the United States. He used to regale us with reminiscences of those earliest days, with a pot under each bed, the contents of which froze some nights, and the outhouse sequestered 'somewhere in the garden.' He may have had misgivings about this return, but his perennial optimism focused him on the young family's singular good fortune. "The war was just over, and there we were with a home of our own," he'd proudly proclaim. The aftermath of the war left lots of things in short supply: Iron radiators, wooden flooring, bath room fixtures. The war effort had focused everyone's attention on the necessities of battle; it would take a while for things to return to a peace-time rhythm. And so with funds borrowed from parents, the conversion of #303 South Main began in earnest, and slowly but surely the house was becoming livable, at least to post-war standards.

Night after summer night, Mom and Dad often accompanied by Dad's parents and Aunt Kate would work by kerosene lamp light, stripping multiple layers of wallpaper from walls, painting woodwork, and removing layer upon layer of carpet, linoleum, and insulating newspaper. The house had no bathroom, as I indicated, just a toilet in a tiny space under the stairs, destined in time to become a closet. There was no central heating, just a pot-bellied stove in the most-frequented room. There was running water, cold only, in a large, black trough sink in the kitchen, where a huge black range sufficed for cooking as well as for auxiliary heating. The outside of the house's foundation had been insulated with the banked ashes of years on end. Repairs, whenever and wherever such, both had been done in the proverbial manner of a wandering tinker. The lawns and gardens wept for attention, though fully a quarter-acre had been plowed into a vegetable garden.

Into this vaguely idyllic picture, there must be introduced some modicum of reality. In that summer of 1945, my mother was pregnant with their second child, my brother, John. I had just turned four years old. My father, though full of goodwill and the best of intentions, knew absolutely nothing about either house repairs or gardening. Totally undaunted, the work progressed. Mom advised and helped with the planting and, eventually, they harvested an enormous quantity of every imaginable vegetable known to them. Dad had planted with a novice's enthusiasm, and for weeks that autumn he would leave for work each morning with a bushel basket of offerings for any willing takers. Cucumbers were pickled; green beans and tomatoes were 'canned'; potatoes and carrots were 'laid down' in the cellar, and zucchinis by the dozen left South Main Street to feed the willing hungry and to reduce the simply overwhelming surplus. The next summer, another garden, though smaller and more disciplined, was planted, but Mom was pregnant again, this time with Margaret, and she suggested that with two near-infants she probably wouldn't be of much help as the 'hired hand' the next summer. Thus our experimental agricultural station came to an end, but its memory and its stories went on for years in Dad's reminiscing and retelling.

None of the real work of readying the house would have been possible without the efforts of one Jim Smith, an instructor at Putnam Technical School, and better known to me as Uncle Jim. (God forbid an adult be addressed by his first name!) He had offered a kind of barter: If Dad would supply the materials and be willing to accept the work of supervised novices, Jim would see the project through to completion. Uncle Jim would arrive each day with a worthy crew of students, transforming the 'inheritance' into a livable space. By the late fall of 1945, we settled down to await the baby's birth, predicted for January, cozy if still a bit uneasy in all the newness.

From Uncle Jim I learned an early lesson in the meaning of paradox, that is, something, which on first glance seems totally foolish, yet which, on further thought, reflection, and experience proves itself to be very sensible. One afternoon, as the crew got ready to call it a day, I was mesmerized to see Uncle Jim and the boys washing their dirty hands at a newly installed outside spigot. But instead of soap, they washed with DIRT (my description for the pile of sand nearby the spigot). They'd wet their hands, apply a good dollop of sand, and then scrub, allowing the abrasive to do its job and lift the accumulated paint and varnish and dirt. Not known to be overly shy, I approached Uncle Jim and questioned the wisdom of washing dirty hands with dirt. Smilingly and patiently, he demonstrated how the sand detached the adhering dirt. I was amazed and duly reported this discovered magic to any and all who'd listen. Lots of things could clean up messy dirt, even dirt itself – so long as it was sand!

In July 1967, just before the day of ordination for me, a gift arrived in from Florida, from Uncle Jim and his wife, Marion. Neatly ensconced in the box, in its own glassine bag, was a handful of beach sand and the simple message: "Remember?" In July 1989, that same sand was sprinkled on Dad's coffin, with the words: "Remember! Earth to earth, ashes to ashes, and dust to dust."

Years later, Dad would recall those early days and ask: "Can you imagine what we felt? There we were, married just five years, with you just turned four, a horrible war winding down, the nation's and the world's economies uncertain, but a second baby on the way, and we OWNED our own home, on three-quarters of an acre of land. We were the luckiest people in the world! God was very good to us, and I don't think I'll ever forget that feeling of being so fortunate, so blessed."

Throughout the forty-eight years that we shared life together, Dad reiterated that theme of 'blessedness' over and over again. No matter what the circumstances (and there were some that we saw as less 'blessed' than others!), Dad saw and spoke of 'blessing.' Life for him was a genuine gift, and most of what life had to offer was perceived and gratefully received as a gift of life, a blessing (even if sometimes in disguise!). After his defeat in the elections of 1954, when he had run for the office of Lieutenant Governor with Abraham Ribicoff, he was asked by the newly elected governor to become the governor's executive aide. [In 1954, the gubernatorial and lieutenant gubernatorial candidates ran separately and not as in later years as a team.] Abraham Ribicoff was the sole Democrat elected to constitutional office that year, and so, understandably, he sought assistance from his own party, and who was more natural than his former running mate? The annual salary as an aide to the governor was about fifteen thousand dollars (as was the governor's) and three times greater than the salary of the Lieutenant Governor. It wasn't hard for Dad to glean the blessing in that situation! The defeat at the polls was yet again a 'blessing' for which we were to be forever grateful. In later years, the blessing would come back to bite him when he successfully gained the office of Lieutenant Governor, leaving behind the fifteen-thousand-dollar salary for the statutorily-set five thousand dollars one. But because he was Lieutenant Governor in January of 1961, when Governor Ribicoff resigned the governorship to join President John Kennedy's cabinet, Dad succeeded automatically to the governorship (and a return to that fifteen-thousand-dollar salary AND a car AND a house). The blessings had returned several-fold, and Dad was no slacker in pointing this fact out to the rest of the family. The blessings were always there; the rest of us just had to get used to finding them and seeing them for what they really were.

I have wracked my brain to come up with those things, which I sense most clearly, most distinctly as long-lasting contributions my father made to my developing life. In trying to categorize them, three major themes seem to play consistently and palpably. Apologizing for the rather lack of luster language, these three are: (1) Constant support of independence; (2) appreciating the innate value of knowing one's roots; (3) knowing that real pain is a factor of life, but that greater pain often comes indirectly rather than directly.

For six long years, while I was a student at Saint Thomas Seminary in Bloomfield, it was Dad's chore, more often than not, to drive me back to school, often on a Sunday night, after a vacation from the books. I don't think there ever was a time when he didn't say to me, and usually without variation, as we wended our way up that long driveway: "Remember, if you're not happy here…if this isn't for you; come home. There's no shame in having tried." No one can imagine the relief, the assurance, the confidence-building in those words, spoken to a teenager. I was just fourteen when I left home for the seminary, and throughout the next twelve years, I always carried those words deep within, and I remained assured that 'home' always awaited me, whenever I chose to return. The decision clearly was mine, but the backup was always there. In many ways, those words and their assurance became the backbone of my independence. I would make the choices, and that freedom of choice would be supported unequivocally. Over the years, I certainly have made choices with which Dad was not thrilled. But never did his support for me and for my choosing waiver. Unlike many parents of friends and acquaintances, he never confused the line between discussion, and even disagreement, about possible choices and the unquestioning support of my freedom of choice. Once made, the choices were mine, and they were accorded the respect due to them as mine. I would guess that each of the four of us, his children, could cite personal examples and tell similar if differing stories, But the bottom line, I would guess, would be the same: We chose, and he supported.

Some years after his retirement from public life, he did an interview with a state newspaper. Somewhere in the discussion, a question must have arisen about the Dempsey children and what life had been like for them growing up as the Governor's children. Implicit in the reporter's view of things was the misunderstanding that each of the four of us had been shaped and formed in some kind of standardized format or parentally-determined fashion, one befitting the state's First Family. Dad didn't argue the point extensively, but at some later point, he said to me that he could not for the life of him understand the reporter's point of view. "Just look at the four of you," he said excitedly. "You're all so very different, one from the other. You've all done what you wanted to do with your lives. When you wanted and how you wanted. And that's how it should be! Where did that guy get the idea that you're all the same?" And he was right – on all counts! Far from being the stereotypes presumed by the reporter, each of us had become his or her own individual person. Sure, we share a lot of the similarities of the same sibling pool, but I would venture to guess that these are far more products of individual choice than they are results of any kind of imposed conformity. We have become four independent adults, whose choices are and have been our own, and Dad's support for this freedom of choice has never been in question. I believe that that is exactly what Dad always had in mind. So implicit was his commitment to both his children's independence and his support of them that to say or even to presume otherwise was totally incomprehensible to him. It's hard for me to imagine a healthier parental commitment or a less stereotypical response from an Irish Catholic father. And yet, such were his!

For us, at least in our growing up years, Irish and Catholic were probably seen and spoken as one word. Irish Protestants and Irish Jews have existed, both here and in Ireland, for centuries, but we wouldn't realize that for years to come. In much the same way, it came as a somewhat mystifying and terrifying thought for me to have to realize that people could be both Catholic and Republican. Mary Benoit, a neighbor, and fellow eldest child in her family, mentioned one day that her parents were Republicans. Naturally, I refuted any such claim by stating the obvious: "But, Mary, your parents are Catholic; they can't be Republicans! It isn't possible!" After all, in our small town at least, it was clear; the line had been drawn: Catholic and Democrat, Protestant (or, as we used to say, non-Catholic), and Republican. People just didn't go around willy-nilly changing what evidently had been ordained. Without ever knowing it, Mary had initiated for me a life-long process of rooting out misperceptions, misunderstandings, and memes. Dad must have been more than slightly amused when I retold the story at the dinner table, but he was quick to set me straight, confirming that Mary Benoit was quite correct and that her parents, and indeed many folks, were both Catholic and Republicans. And then with a broad smile, he added: "Poor souls!"

Irish and Catholic in a French Canadian mill town, where the one local Catholic church was pastored and staffed firstly by Dutch priests and then by French Canadian priests provided its own often less than subtle eccentricities. For us, and in my grandparents' parlance, the priests with Polish-sounding names (like Gajewski and Gadarowski, Gubala, Konopka, and Wodarski) were considered the 'Irish priests,' because they, like us, spoke English as a first language. Or, at least, French wasn't their first or usual language. In adulthood, I came to marvel at my ancestors' faith commitment, which impelled them to Sunday Mass, without fail, even when the liturgy was in incomprehensible Latin, and the sermons and announcements, as often as not, were in equally indiscernible French.

There was the Irish-American Club, the site of annual Saint Patrick's Day dinners, and the place which served as the local venue for card games and political 'discussions,' and general socializing. But, for the most part, the home was the soil from which our dual roots of Irish and Catholic sprang. Of course, we were Democrats as well and had been since the days of naturalization, but Irish Catholics somehow most adequately defined our essence and our daily lives. Saint Mary's was our parish church, and when the time came, Saint Mary's was our parish school, where the French language (as practiced by Canadians) once again held sway. Kindergarten was no Nursey School! Sister Ann Felix was a teacher and not just a manager of some sixty-five-year-olds. And teach she did: Numbers, cursive handwriting, catechism, and, yes, French! Imagine the look on Dad's face when, at the supper table one evening, when asked about what we had learned in school that day, this proud five-year-old sang: *"Trempes ton pain, Marie, trempes ton pain, Marie, trempes ton pain dans la sauce."* Pleading eyes sought out my mother's response to: "Any idea what they're up to at that school?" [Though she often doesn't seem to remember it herself, it's probably a good place and time to disclose that my mother is NOT Irish; she is in fact of German and French Canadian descent. Her father was born in the area of Baden-Baden, Germany, and her mother was a native of Cape Breton Island, Nova Scotia, Canada, of French heritage. My mother's confusion about her own ethnic background stems from the fact that she 'hung around with them ('the Irishers') for all those years!"]

My entire childhood was literally filled with stories of life in Ireland, and, at least in my youngest years, Tipperary was just another state, Cahir another Putnam, Ireland another place where my father and his parents had once lived. Most of my grandparents' friends were, like them, immigrants from Ireland. And while I occasionally misunderstood or forgot that 'braces' were actually 'suspenders' or that a 'vest' was really nothing more than an 'undershirt' and that a 'jumper' was better known in America as a 'sweater,' I must confess that the Cork and Kerry accents of some of those friends threw me for a loop. When Mrs. Toolan or Mr. Hannifan spoke excitedly, I was lost. It was as if English had been abandoned for some strange Celtic tongue to which my ear was a stranger. I must have complained of this to my grandmother one day, and she gently explained to me that, unlike she and Grampy, those people from Cork and Kerry had a much tougher time shedding the Irish brogue, and that even she, at times, had trouble understanding all that they said. She and my grandfather, coming from Tipperary and Dublin respectively, experienced no such problems in being understood in this country because they had no trace of brogue, only, perhaps, a slight accent. Or so they firmly believed! Periodically, Dad betrayed his linguistic roots, eliminating a 'th' from where it belonged or adding a 'th' to where it didn't. The best example I recall is the word 'throat,' which, on occasion, exited his mouth as 'troath.' His ear usually didn't even catch the malapropism, any more than his mother did when she coached our diction with the instruction to "put your tongue between your teeth and say 'tunder.'"

Linguistically and philosophically, the Irish inserted itself into our daily lives in time-worn ways. The farewell, 'good night,' would be hallowed by the additional 'and God bless!' And almost any prediction of the future would be conditioned by the words 'God willing.' What they said and how they said it were traditionally Irish and Catholic. But Dad was never content to allow his essence to be reduced solely to words. He remembered with sad anger the newspapers' Help Wanted ads, which closed with the despicable words 'Irish need not apply!' He rejoiced in an Irish identity, and he identified strongly with being a Catholic. Going to church on Sunday or a holyday was never described as an obligation or a duty; it simply was what an Irish Catholic did on those occasions. It was as central to life and life's happiness as were the elements, the seasons, or the human emotions. What one IS defines what one DOES. How many Communion Breakfast groups, from Thompson to Greenwich, heard him declaim unabashedly: "If you want to set the example for others, then be that example yourself." Words, as crucial as they might be, could never be enough. The true test of a person, he believed, was the living of the words spoken, the doing of the deeds foretold, the keeping of the promises made.

Such was the world in which we grew up as youngsters and as young adults. Some might call it provincial and insular, but it was a world in which we rarely doubted, seldom questioned, and never wondered about who we were and what we were meant to do in life. We knew who we were and what was expected of us. So when I hear behaviorists and psychologists exalting stability and security and self-knowledge, I look back and give thanks for the parental heritage that is ours.

Pain was never a welcome visitor in Dad's life; he never wore it like a badge of courage. Perhaps because he had remarkably good health for seventy-four years and lived relatively free of physical limitation, he never developed a 'close relationship' with discomfort and pain, nor did he ever develop an especially thick skin to guard against it. And so when the pain came, it arrived unbidden and unwelcome. And, believe me, there was pain.

In the winter of 1959-1960, Dad joined a group of local basketball players, who were involved in a local fundraising project for Saint Joseph High School in neighboring North Grosvenordale. He was then in his mid-forties (an age at which, he would later say he should have known better, but...), and he had not played sports competitively for years. Undaunted, he was one of the starting five. Mom says that she barely got herself situated in the bleachers when play began. Within minutes, if not seconds, whistles shrilled, and Dad was down, unable to rise without assistance, and experiencing visible pain. He had torn his right calf muscle, and he would be on crutches, in physical therapy, and on medication for ensuing months. Completely unused to 'sitting around and doing nothing,' he was far from an ideal patient. When, at last, he was able to go back to work in Hartford, he was still unable to drive. Enter the inevitable, though invisible, 'blessing.' State Police at the Danielson Barracks assigned a trooper to drive Dad to and from the Capitol for the duration. Enter the 'blessing in disguise' in the person of one Vin McSweeney, who, though not quite 'angelic,' would pick him up at home in Putnam and deposit him at the office in Hartford each morning and then return him home each evening. Initially embarrassed at having to be chauffeured, it wasn't long before Dad found that he could accomplish a fair amount of work in the car during these two hours of the daily commute. "See," he would remind us; "if it hadn't been for that leg, I never would have known how to work and drive at the same time!" From that time onward, he and Vin (or Vince or Mac) McSweeney were almost inseparable. Initially, on crutches and then on an ungainly cane, he and his driver would make their way from car to desk, and again later from desk to car. [From the window of a study hall at the seminary, I caught my first glimpse of Dad incapacitated. Tears welled up as I saw that even the unbeatable could be beaten, temporarily, even the healthy could be stymied, for the moment, and even a hero could limp.] Years later, well after he became governor, Vin continued to drive him whenever he was at home in Eastern Connecticut, especially during the summers at Lake Alexander.

Despite the relative absence of physical pain, there was a pain in life nonetheless. I don't think Dad ever became immune to negative newspaper articles or negative criticism that bordered on the personal. His human sensitivity often amazed more hardened colleagues and caused some of them to wonder how or if this guy could last in the sometimes raucous and disparaging political arena. But, by far, the most effective means by which to cause him real pain was to cause pain or distress to his wife or to his children. The mere suggestion was enough to bring color to his face and near stony rage to his voice. He accepted that a public person could be 'fair (if offended) game.' But, the family was something else altogether; they were not fair game in any way whatsoever. And God help anyone who failed to get that message, loud and clear.

Each of the four of us has stories that continue to color our perspectives on our growing-up and school years. The rector of the seminary (an Irish Catholic and Republican, no doubt) seemed to me to be overly zealous in assuring that I received no special treatment because of my father. My movements seemed inordinately monitored, my infractions meticulously punished, and my occasional requests scrupulously scrutinized. When Dad was to be inaugurated as Lieutenant Governor, in January of 1959, I had hoped to be allowed to join the rest of the family for the day's festivities. No such luck! I would be allowed to be present for the actual administration of the oath of office, but presence at and participation in that evening's Governor's Ball was most assuredly beyond the pale of consideration. Somehow I did manage to include the noon's luncheon as part of the oath-taking, but I was back, safely on 'holy ground' by afternoon's end. The rector never mentioned those events, never inquired how things had gone, and never showed any interest whatsoever in what was happening in my family. However, two years later, in January of 1961, as Dad prepared to take the oath as Connecticut's Governor, I again had to approach that same rector with a now-familiar request. The events were to be few and of a low-key nature. The rector smacked me with his breviary book, reminding me that he had been quite lenient 'the last time,' and that in my request I was 'making a habit of this!' I went; I returned before dinner; the rector never again referred to the events.

My brother John was the only one of us apparently interested in competitive sports, and he was good at it.

Whether his playing time was ever commensurate with his athletic ability remains a mystery. Carefulness about not showing preference or playing favorites probably cost him more time on the court or field than his abilities ever did. Later in life, his name certainly gave him near-instantaneous recognition and equally quick suspicion. Though he had been born and raised in Eastern Connecticut, his decision to seek the Democratic nomination for Congress from the Second Congressional District earned him labels of carpetbagger and opportunist. His success in gaining the nomination was contested, and he lost the Primary election. Later news-making events, emanating from his business dealings, were fueled by constant reference to his father, and allegations suddenly assumed the validity of fact. You don't or shouldn't expect special treatment because of your name, but you certainly don't want or deserve to be penalized because of it either. But not everyone sees it that way, apparently.

At Northwest Catholic High School, Margaret and Kevin seemed consistently held to a 'higher standard' of academic prowess and human behavior. The then principal of that august institution seemed cut from the very same cloth as the seminary rector and probably espoused many of the same mindsets. Margaret was reminded, and not just once, that 'just because your father's the Governor,' no slack would be cut for her; in fact, less often was. Detentions were plentiful even when prior notification had been given. I'm thinking of one particular instance where Dad had arranged for Margaret to accompany him to Groton Airport, there to interview Jacqueline Kennedy for an article in the school's newspaper. The school was alerted to her proposed absence, and her article won her yet another detention, because 'just because your father's the Governor that doesn't mean...'" The only detention period which I ever remember hearing that she escaped was thanks to the personal appearance of one Danny Thomas at the Northwest Catholic school office, where he simply and naively said that he had come to pick Margaret up and take her home. The office staff swooned and ran to get Margaret out of the detention study hall. I often wonder what got said to that clerical staff afterward. The principal was sure to have had choice words!

In the summer following his sixteenth birthday, Kevin was 'seen' driving a car in a less than acceptable manner. Despite the fact that he was neither present at the site of the alleged violation nor driving the type of car described, the failure of law enforcement to charge him was yet further 'evidence' of the preferential treatment meted out to the Governor's children. Teen years are rarely easy years, but they can be made even harder when people choose to make them so. The treatment accorded may have been preferential but only in the most distortedly perverse way!

If Dad never dealt easily with criticism or prejudice or false accusation aimed at him, he dealt even less well when his wife or children were the targets. I believe that anyone who really knew him knew equally well that the fastest and the most effective way to give Dad pain was to cause pain to his family. Perceived injustice against his children could send him into a near rage. Genuine unhappiness on Mom's part could put him on the brink of resignation from office. Lies, allegations, and accusations against his family could transform this peaceful man into someone few of his colleagues would recognize. And yet, in very rare cases did he ever take our part overtly or publicly. The far more usual was for him to acknowledge to us the unfairness of the situation, to apologize that we were being targeted because of him, and then explain why nothing further would be said or done to vindicate us. "In life, you have to choose your battles carefully; you've got to be smart. You never want to get into a pissing contest with a skunk; he'll out-piss you every time." On reflection, this said a great deal about our father and the kind of person he was. But it probably said even more about the characters of the opponents!

In the early sixties, not too long after the family had moved to Hartford, the State Police became concerned about recently unearthed threats made against the Dempsey children. We were, after all, fairly visible, with all of us attending area schools, with readily predictable schedules, and well-known routes of travel. We were very obvious in our usualness, and we were eminently findable. Commissioner Mulcahy apprised Dad of their findings and urged him to take these seriously. Dad never had anything but the greatest respect for the Commissioner, both as a professional and as a person, so there was no argument, just sad acceptance of what would be necessary. Security at the Residence was increased, with State Troopers on duty at all times. Transportation was transferred to the Troopers as well, and any unusual events were to be reported immediately. For months, Dad's preoccupation with security was never far from him, and his manner betrayed both worry and angry alert. This was not the life he had anticipated, and it certainly was not the life we had left behind in Putnam. It was only after many uneventful months that his manner relaxed, and he allowed himself a return to normalcy. But, literally to his dying day, his greatest vulnerability was his family, and his strongest urge was to be the protector of them all. As his days slipped away, whenever I got ready to leave him, in his room at the Farmington hospital, which bears his name, I'd lean over and kiss him and say: "Bye, Dad; I love you."

Without fail or hesitation, he'd respond: "I love you too; I love you all." Even to the end, it was clearly important to him that each member know and that all members recognize that he was Dad…to and for us all.

Very often, I'm afraid, we are tempted to take the measure of a man by the size of the inheritance he leaves behind, and, more often than not, that size is preceded by a dollar sign. Dad was never, I'm convinced, seduced by money. Oh, he knew its value all right, and he respected and appreciated its potential. But he never craved it, and he certainly never idolized it. He would laugh at the thought of his leaving an inheritance, except to the extent that he felt a strong obligation to provide for Mom's security. Apart from that, the legacy was a kind of joke. He'd laughingly comment: "If I had my way, Mom and I would spend the last red cent we had the day before we died, leaving nothing, owing no one."

But when all is said and done, we, his heirs, are the wealthiest people imaginable. We have inherited from him independence as persons, rootedness in our individual and family identity, and conviction that our pain was his greatest pain. As the jingle in the ad asks: "Who could ask for anything more?"

Remembering A Husband and Wife

Mom and Dad on election night, 1966

It must have been in January of 1934 that they met. She was a new girl, a recent arrival, joining the freshman class mid-term. He was a senior, cutting quite the figure as a stand-out 'jock,' acknowledged as outstanding in football, basketball, and track. She was fifteen; he had just turned nineteen. She was just arriving; he was on the verge of graduating. And for the next fifty-five and a half years, they would remain 'an item,' preeminently ordinary in so many ways, extraordinarily unusual in others.

Mom's family had come to Putnam because her father had found a job at Bloom's, a local silk mill in the Rhodesville section of town. A first-generation American of French-Canadian and German ancestry, Mary Frey was the third of five children born to Carl Albert Frey and Margaret Sampson. The family settled into a small rented house on Killingly Avenue, next door to Richard's Dairy, a popular spot for Putnam teens, but seriously removed from the downtown area by a healthy walk of about two miles. The necessity of walking would only get worse with time, for, later, the Freys would move into another rented house, this time in Sawyer's District, near the County Children's Home, probably closer to three miles from the downtown area. If one is to believe the stories told, it was not unusual for Dad to walk out to the Frey's to pick Mom up for a movie, walk with her into town, walk her home after the movie, and finally walk back home to Church Street. No wonder he was such an athletic figure! And one can't help but surmise that parents felt a certain security in all that open-air walking!

From January 1934 to December 1936, they 'kept company.' Despite distances, seasons, and schedules, they managed to see one another on a more or less regular basis. Then in December 1936, the Freys were on the move again this time from Putnam to Malden, Massachusetts, a really impossible 'walk,' even for an athletic twenty-one-year-old! Bloom's had closed, and so Grampa Frey was once again on the road in search of another, increasingly elusive job in the textile industry. Thus began a period of 'borrowed cars' and 'weekend visits.' Eventually, on July 27, 1940, they were married at Saint Mary's Church in Warren, Rhode Island, where her grandmother, Martina Frey, had her home and where Mom was living at that time.

As we, their children, got older and became understandably and naturally more interested and curious about our parents as sweethearts, they took a more than a fair amount of gentle ribbing about their six-year courtship. Dad usually got saddled with the accusation of 'not being able to make up his mind,' while Mom was cast as 'the much younger woman' who couldn't be swept off her feet, even by the smilingly handsome and gregarious Irishman. Others would contribute that the major problem wasn't so much age as it was the prospect of a 'mixed marriage.' After all, wool did not marry silk and vice versa! There was sparse and sporadic evidence that Dad may have had 'other interests' along the way, an accusation which he strongly denied. But, one day, probably in the 1950s, my sister, Margaret, found a small, pocket-sized, black leather address book. From its inscription, it was clear that the book had been a gift from Mary Frey, whose name alphabetically therein was amplified with the code '#1.' Yet under various other alphabetical headings, other names and addresses appeared, oddly enough, all of them female. My sister had found Dad's proverbial 'Little Black Book!' However, when my grandmother found my sister gleeful and giggly with her discovery, Nana Dempsey could not get it back from her. At last, in maternal desperation, she assured my sister that the contents of that 'little black book' could be of no possible interest to her or to anyone else because the names and addresses were simply those of 'old absentee ballot voters.'

Nice try, Nana, but what about those addresses in England and Ireland? Old absentee ballot voters? Yah, sure!!!

On a more serious note, I remember asking Mom, later in life, about that six-year courtship. She was readily forthcoming. She shared that it was really Dad's decision that carried the day. If they were going to marry, then they would do it 'right.' That meant: A steady and dependable job; buying a car; having sufficient funds in the bank; having furniture laid away and paid for 'on time' before the fact, being reasonable and responsible. If Dad was anything, and apparently so from a young age, he was responsibility personified, and he would remain so all his life-long. He had been taught, and taught well, that there is no such thing as a 'right' without a concomitant 'responsibility.' He could have whatever he could afford; borrowing was a foreign notion. And so, odd as it may seem today, our parents never even had a mortgage until 1970, the year before he left office, when they bought the house in Mumford Cove, Groton.

In some ways, I suppose, the Freys were indeed the veritable 'gypsy.' They had moved from Warren, Rhode Island, to Pawtucket, where Mom was born; from Pawtucket to Lowell, Massachusetts; from Lowell to Putnam, Connecticut; from Putnam to Malden, Massachusetts; and, finally, back to the Warren area. In many ways, the Freys played out, in their meanderings, one of the most common human and literary themes: Struggling to leave 'home;' succeeding at last, but eventually returning 'home' in the end. But the Dempseys, in stark contrast, had settled in Putnam, there to live and work and die (in the very same house!) from 1926 to 1961. Responsibility and stability are two pillars on which a 'good life' could be built. And so it was!

As history is wont to do, it repeated itself. Mom and Dad, after a honeymoon in the White Mountains, settled on Bradley Street in Putnam. They would not leave northeastern Connecticut until Inauguration Day 1961, only to return in November of 1988, nine months before Dad's death. Perhaps there is a lot more to be learned from popular sayings about the human proclivity to live in and to repeat cycles: "What goes around comes around."

"You meet the same people coming down the ladder as you passed going up."

"All life is a circle." Certainly, the repetition of cycles is evident in many families, and children might just learn a bit about themselves and their own futures by getting to know the stories of their parents and grandparents.

One of the very best aspects of coming from a relatively small place is the possibility, every once in a while, of being afforded glimpses of parents through other peoples' eyes. Not so very long ago, Henry Girard, who had been in high school with Mom and Dad, told me that he had the clearest recollection of the day that Mary Frey came onto the scene at Putnam High. He went on: "We all saw that look on John Dempsey's face, and we knew that it was all over." Whether they were psychic or just good guessers, they were proved right. For whatever reason, my guess is that there was never any other serious romantic interest for either of them from that time forward. But this is not to say that there weren't other 'interested (and interesting) parties' on the local scene. Mom remembers quite clearly a day when Al Turcotte, who rode the same bus as Mom, apologetically admitted that he would like very much to carry her books for her, but that he had been warned off. "By whom ?" she wanted to know.

"John got word to me through some of his friends," Al admitted. The very next morning, at the first opportunity presented, she had a word with John in the hallway, assuring him that he may be a sports hero, but that she could manage her own life, quite well, thank you! She was always short in stature, but that never stood in the way of her self-determination. She may not have then recognized the word 'chutzpah,' but she had it!

In time, a distance would be complicating; human foibles would create problems; personalities would need curbing, but the initial attraction would mature into a relationship that spanned the next fifty-five and a half years. Simply in terms of longevity, that kind of relationship inspires, variously, both awe and skepticism. In view of contemporary experience, I guess that the skeptics deserve their doubts. However, as Dempsey children, we have never shared them. Ours has been the awe and the very real fright, that such a legacy engenders. It is an inheritance both comforting and simultaneously disquieting. We were born into, and we grew up in an atmosphere of amazing stability, one on which we have always counted, one which we never doubted. But to be handed that as a 'model' or a legacy to be replicated…that is an awesome and frightening gift!

When we were children, our parents delighted us (and probably took equal delight themselves) by playing a game, which they called by no particular name, and which they would heartily aver was no 'game' at all. Rather, it was purported to be an exhibit of almost magical 'mind-reading.' Dad would get one of the four of us silently to choose an object in the room, and, invariably, Mom would be able to guess what it was that Dad was holding or pointing to or even thinking about. Driven to near distraction, we would beg and plead to know how they did it. But it was all to no avail! We would accuse them of using surreptitious eye contact, and so Mom would be blindfolded. We would assume that it was voice modulation, and so Dad would be forced to speak in monotone. We would assume that it was a barely detectable hand gesture, and so Mom would be sent into another room. Try as we might, we could never find the 'trick,' and they would eagerly assure us that it was no trick; it was the genuine article, the science of mind-reading. To this day, not one of the four of us can explain how it was done, but not so many years ago, we were convinced that these parents of ours were formidable foes of any secret thought or deed, and, most of the time, we acted accordingly! After all, what sensible kid was going to take a chance when, just maybe, they really could read minds!

The truly amazing thing that happened, over the many years they were together, was that they became really adept at knowing what the other was thinking or feeling. They could, and did on occasion, finish each other's sentences. They knew without the limitations of language, or so it seemed, what the other was experiencing. They could tell what was about to happen, and they could enjoy the simplicity of communication without the baggage of words.

Never was that truer than in the last days of Dad's life. Though frustrated with the necessary inactivity, which a hospital ambiance compels, they seemed truly content just being together in the same room, at the same time. Sometimes they'd watch television; sometimes Mom would read cards and notes and letters from concerned friends and associates; other times there was nothing but the language of silent presence, and that seemed sufficient for both of them. And to borrow from Simon and Garfunkel, the memories of their fifty-five plus years together 'echoed in the sounds of silence.' I asked Mom, after Dad's death, if they had ever talked together about his dying. She paused as if reacting to a strange, unanticipated question, and then said: "No! We both knew what was happening (and how could she not since she had been the one to share the dire prognosis with him!); we couldn't do anything about it, so what was the good of talking?" Undaunted by this wisdom, I pushed for what I thought should have been discussed, or, at least spoken.

"I did ask him one day, "she said, "if he were afraid." "About all this," he queried, gesturing toward the oxygen and the intravenous lines? "No," he continued; I'm only afraid for you!" He worried about her; she worried about him. That's the way, apparently, it had ever been, and so why would it be any different at life's end? Their togetherness had seen them through a lot of living, and now it would see them through this wrenching transition.

In all probability, Dad was considered by many as ethnically sentimental. After all, aren't all Irishmen? And yet, few people ever divined the true depth and breadth of his emotions, especially as these pertained to our mother. A couple of extremely telling examples spring to mind: Somewhere there is a photograph of Dad, taken seconds after he took the oath of office as Governor, for the first time, in January of 1961. In the photo, he has just turned from Chief Justice Baldwin, and with his right hand still upraised, his index finger and thumb form the usual sign of approbation and looking at Mom, he smiles knowingly. As we later reviewed the photos, I asked him what was going on in his head at that particular moment. I should have guessed! "For the very first time in twenty-one years of marriage, I knew with certainty that she would be OK. If I were to drop dead that instant, she would have a pension (one half his fifteen thousand dollars a year salary) for the rest of her life." Much of his life, both emotional and material, is summed up in that gesture and in those words. They had each come from very humble means, where futures were rarely insured, and where pensions were almost unknown. And yet, here he was at age forty-six, for the first time in his life, sure of his wife's future. Much has been written of the joy of that day when the immigrant became Connecticut's Chef Executive. But the real joy of that day lay elsewhere for Dad; it lay in the assurance of the future, a promise of well-being, insurance against his absence, not for him but for his wife. The joys and the burdens of the governorship would occupy many of his thoughts and his days, but right now, at the very beginning, the focus of that joy was elsewhere. "I knew that she would be OK, whatever happened to me from that point forward."

Much later, in the summer of 1989, after he had been diagnosed with untreatable small-cell lung cancer, and on more than one occasion, he cautioned me not to let Mom forget about 'the box' they had. But when I asked her, she seemed to have no idea what that meant. At last, I told him that we were at a loss about 'the box.' Looking at me as if I were failing the role of the 'eldest son,' he confided that there was a bank box, about which Mom was obviously forgetting, and in that box, there was a Knights of Columbus life insurance policy. "It's not for much," he continued, "but it'll take care of 'certain expenses.' She'll know what that means." And so, even in the very last days of his life, his overarching concerns were for Mom and any possible burdens of financing his funeral. His solicitude was simple and genuine; he was a husband, and husbands were to 'take care of things,' right down to the very last, it seems.

Despite popular perceptions (often based more on appearances than on realities) and misconceptions, the family's finances were extremely ordinary. People tend to forget that for most of Dad's ten years as Governor, his salary was fifteen thousand dollars a year, as set by law. Granted there was the gracious living afforded by The Residence, but family expenses did not stop with household considerations. By 1966, for example, there were three college students in the family simultaneously. My memory serves me poorly when it comes to remembrances of finances. In fact, memory alone would tend to convince me that money was never an issue in our household. But conventional reasoning would say differently. Surely there must have been times when money was short when things were 'tight,' but Mom and Dad must have been extremely quiet in that regard. I do, however, remember one incident which might have been a reflection of other conversations they had had 'between just them.' In sorting and opening the day's mail at The Residence, Mom found a letter thanking Dad for a recent speaking engagement at a Communion Breakfast. Enclosed was a generous check, an honorarium for the early Sunday morning in a distant parish. After lunch, Dad reviewed the mail as Mom sat nearby. He read the letter approvingly, looked at the check, turned it over, and endorsed it, payable to the sender. Mom, as if resuming some prior discussion, detailed how many things could have been done with the speaking fees, which Dad consistently refused to accept. As if reiterating a new won point, Dad countered: "I've never accepted a fee, and I don't intend to start now. We've managed so far without them, and we'll be fine. Don't worry. They need the money more than we do. I'll have Eileen (his secretary) send it back." That glimpse, for that indeed was all it was, that glimpse affords me an inkling that money and finances were, at least sometimes, a worry for them, as they are for all people. It's just that we heard little if anything about them, and so we grew up never fully realizing that our parents, like thousands of other folks throughout the state had sporadic struggles 'making ends meet.' Dad's detachment from money's allure is, at least in retrospect, inspiring. Yet, I doubt somehow that that was the word that Mom would have used back then!

To say that Mom occupied the center of Dad's life seems a bit trite and minimalist, and yet other descriptions fall equally short of the mark. He seemed never fully content, never wholly himself, if she were not near. On countless nights, despite her rational arguments, he would drive home to Putnam or the lake (Killingly), rather than stay alone in Hartford or somewhere on the road. He would counter with the seemingly self-serving excuse: "I'll sleep better at home." That need for nearness and the habit that it engenders seems to have become parts of both of them. When Dad was hospitalized for eye surgery in the late 70s or early 80s, I arrived home on the day of the surgery to find Mom's bed undisturbed and her chair in the living room still warm. When I asked if she had slept, she assured me she had, but her face belied her words. "I just couldn't go to bed; I sat in the chair. You know, I can count on the fingers of my hands the nights we have not been together since we married. I just couldn't go to bed; it wouldn't have worked." My sister, Margaret could tell tales of what it was like being the only one at home with Dad in December of 1966, when Mom was hospitalized for surgery. That he was not himself was clear from his attempts at breakfast-table conversation. That he was not functioning as usual could not be denied in the face of the two socks of different colors, which he sported that day. That he was not managing her absence was clear from his darkened eyes and his empty stares. My first hint about the sudden surgery came in an air-mailed letter which assured me that Mom was fine, and that she'd be home soon, and that I (in far off Paris) should not be worried. It was another day and the arrival of another letter that finally explained what should not frighten me and the very recent impromptu medical discovery and the need for sudden surgery. Dad's 'failure to thrive' in Mom's absence had given me a very uneasy twenty-four hours, wherein ignorance was far from bliss.

Many times over the years before his death, we jocosely used to hope out loud that he would not be left in life without her, for we truly believed that he would never be able to manage without her. And those hopes were favorably realized.

Partnerships, as far as I can tell, presume some kind of mutuality, some kind of equality between partners. Dad was perhaps out of synch with men of his time and tradition because he was, in many concrete ways, a very liberated man. Being accustomed to making decisions for a city or a state never blinded him to the absolute necessity of sharing decisions in a marriage. There were times, doubtless, when spontaneity lost out to strategizing, or when the 'hard sell' was called for, but I think it's fair to say that he never made a decision affecting us, his family, without genuine collaboration with Mom. Nowhere was that more evident than in the decisions made relating to elections and elected offices. Clearly, public and political life was vitally important to Dad. But the decisions about that life, since they touched our family often and importantly, were made with Mom, and it was done very naturally, matter-of-factly, instinctually. It is no revelation to family and friends that politics would never have been Mom's first choice as a lifelong career. But it was Dad's, and that became a crucial piece of the decision-making they undertook. And it was a mutual process, I can assure you. Many people, perhaps particularly among members of the press in 1970 (and in the inner circles of the state's Democratic Party), were convinced that Mom had 'lowered the boom' at long last, thereby decreeing Dad's decision to retire from public life. I think, in all honesty, even we, their children, raised silent doubts about this turn in the road. But nothing could be further from the truth! In his announcement that he would not again be a candidate for the governorship, he talked about this decision as being a family decision, one to which we had all been invited to contribute. And that was perfectly true. But the final decision came from them both. Things had changed perceptibly over the years of the sixties, and, quite frankly, not all of the changes in political life were seen by Dad as desirable. He was convinced that 'a new day' required new leadership, and he was equally convinced that he was not that leader. His discussions with Mom were private, and their decision was shared with us for comment and contribution. There was never any indication that Mom 'had had enough' and was forcing the issue of retirement. Yet the rumors persisted. I asked her one time if there were any truth to the suspicions that she had caused Dad to retire. She was, in my opinion, extremely forthright. "I may be a lot of things, but I have never been crazy. What kind of life would it have been if I had forced him to stop doing what he so clearly loved doing? What kind of peace would we have had if I pressured him to retire before he really wanted to? What we have done, we have always done together. And if he had wanted to run again, he would have, and I would have done what I have always done. I would have been there, wherever he was!"

That kind of 'togetherness,' which characterized this couple, these parents, at least in the eyes of their children, was the usual, the given, for us. So real was our conviction that, in all probability, we were far less prone than many other children even to imagine 'playing one parent off against the other.' Fundamentally, we were convinced that it just wouldn't work; one just didn't act independently of the other. Naturally, this kind of conviction gives children a somewhat warped view of the rest of life, and the rest of the real world. Our friends may have tried (and even succeeded) in the scam of pitting one parent against the other, but we knew, deep down, that it simply wouldn't work for us…not with these two. Even if a presumption that every set of parents in the world were like ours was occasionally exploded, we four derived from that 'togetherness' a definite view of how things OUGHT to be. Parents OUGHT to be together, in every conceivable way. That's what we saw; that's what we lived; the ideal was set immutably.

That kind of 'togetherness' also made some aspects of life a lot easier. Even though we knew that Dad loved fishing, and Mom didn't; even though we knew that Mom loved shopping, and Dad didn't; whenever there was a question of what to get them for their anniversary, or what to give them for Christmas, or how best to celebrate a particular event, the basic rule of thumb was quite simple: Do something that BOTH will enjoy doing, something that BOTH will use, or go somewhere that BOTH will appreciate. In the mid-sixties, as a wedding anniversary gift, I had found a set of key chains, which seemed destined for their use. Dangling from a short silver chain were the figures of a man and a woman, facing one another and holding hands. On the reverse side of the figures were the words: "Ni moi sans toi, ni toi sans moi." Neither you without me nor me without you. Both images and words depicted what we had seen them living.

Depending on your own personal lenses, John and Mary Dempsey could be seen as Governor and First Lady, John and Mary, Mayor and Mrs., neighbors and friends. But for us, it was usually hard to get around what was most obvious and true for us; they were Mom and Dad, and their other incarnations were clearly secondary to our way of seeing things. Despite occasional and youthful musings about what they must have been like as youngsters and sweethearts themselves, we rarely saw them or even thought of them as distinct or separate from 'our parents,' Mom and Dad. I don't know that we ever gave much thought to how they saw each other, what words they would use to describe themselves to and for each other, how they related to one another privately; they were our parents, and that was that! We heard them call one another 'dear' or 'hon,' but even such terms of endearment failed to open our eyes to who they were for one another. Moments after Dad's death, while the nurse and Aunt Margaret, and my brother, John, consoled a bereft wife, Mom revealed what may well have been the essence of their 'togetherness,' their relatedness. Acknowledging with gratitude the comforting words, she said: "He was my best friend…for fifty-five years…my best friend."

It's hard for us, or for any children, I suppose, to acknowledge that parents have an existence apart from being parents. And yet, quite clearly and sensibly, they do! They must! The days of limerance pass; the heat of new romance matures; the roles of parents change; and what is left to the partnership? What holds two people together for over half a century? What is the glue that sustains the attachment when the years' decree decline and the prowess of youth is reduced to memory? 'Friendship' seems like such an understated commodity, such a banal expression. But maybe that's because we overlook the Old English root of the word 'friend,' 'freon,' meaning 'to love.' Perhaps we forget the Christian Scriptures' powerful affirmation:

"...there is no greater love than to lay down one's life for a friend." If a friend is one who is loved, in fact so loved that even death is not too great a price, then 'friendship' surely qualifies as a fitting description of what two people create in terms of human love and bonding.

They were husband and wife for nearly forty-nine years; they were parents most of that time; they were grandparents, neighbors, and lots of other things to lots of other people along the way. But most importantly to them, they were and remained 'best friends' for the whole of their fifty-five years together.

Remembering the Flood
Of 1955 And Beyond

It's hard, if not impossible, to think of Dad without thinking of the flood of 1955 and of the terrible and terrifying devastation it brought to our hometown of Putnam. The Quinebaug River runs some sixty-nine miles from south-central Massachusetts into Connecticut, effectively dividing Putnam in two, before continuing on its way down to the Shetucket and eventually the Thames rivers. As with almost every textile town in New England, the banks of the Quinebaug were lined with mills: Woolen, cotton, silk, fabric, or thread, and nearby were mill-owned housing for the mills' workers. These were usually multi-family units, ranging from duplexes to tenements, more often than not dotting the area's most proximate to the river – not the most fashionable part of town in which to live. Rivers for centuries had been utilized as the most readily available and cheapest form of waste disposal, waste of all kinds from industrial to domestic. In summer, when the water might run low, certain and definite odors of an unpleasant nature would rise into the atmosphere and assault the senses. Tan or gray scuzz would loft off the water into the air, challenging the neighborhood kids to capture the errant 'balloons,' while watchful mothers yelled: "Don't touch that stuff!" You can't help but wonder if memories of living in such close proximity to the Quinebaug would return to Dad in the 1960s, adding to his determination to do something definitive about clean air and clean water in Connecticut. In any case, power to run the mills' machinery demanded a ready and inexpensive source of power, and converting the energy of rapidly moving water to electricity seemed both an obvious and a cheap solution. At the same time, disposal of chemical waste from processes like dyeing cloth and thread was readily at hand, and the rivers' water swept the detritus away from one's own doorstep and downstream, only to deposit it, of course, on someone else's!

In the early morning hours of August 19, 1955, the phone rang at the Mayor's home. The word was not good! Connecticut was in for some very turbulent weather, and Putnam should brace itself for flooding and hurricane winds. Dad left the house shortly after that phone call to take up leadership of what would need to be done. The damage done by the swollen Quinebaug was alarmingly extensive. The city was effectively halved when its three bridges were damaged. Electricity, telephone, and water ceased their flow into homes and businesses. Amid the aftermath, a supply of magnesium exploded, turning the night sky pink for several consecutive nights and showering the town with burned shards. And when morning came, the evidence of those showers was clearly evident, and it was NOT manna! At one point, we didn't see Dad for more than twenty-four hours straight, and although Mom, doubtless, worried about him, I think we all knew that he would be fine and that he really was needed in the thick of things elsewhere. For a man who was not naturally endowed with endless patience, he could become a most patient man in situations needing that virtue. We have been told that he spent precious and countless moments coaxing older residents from their homes, reassuring them that they would be cared for, and that, if it weren't truly necessary, he wouldn't be asking them to leave it all. Usually successful with his persuasive skills, his powers did not always prevail, however, and in those cases, with visible risk to all concerned, residents would have to be removed, sometimes bodily, from the roofs of their now-inundated houses in the large amphibious machines, dubbed 'ducks.' On at least several occasions, Dad reminisced: "If I could have got my hands on Gus Giraca, I would have throttled him." You see, Mr. Giraca and his sons had refused to leave their home. Instead, as the water rose, they moved up, until, at last, they were stranded on the roof and had to be rescued! From the top of a mud pile nearly fourteen feet high, you could reach out and touch the top of the Southern New England Telephone Company (just opposite the post office on Main Street). What once had been the city's major thoroughfare was now a murky lake, whose brackish waters occasionally afforded glimpses of submerged rooftops, the vestiges of downtown homes and businesses. The Irish-American Club's building on Pomfret Street was neatly and accurately cloven in two. On what had been one of its second-floor inside walls, one could now see framed photos and citations, shifting in the August breeze. Jules Home Furnishings and Appliances remained, but one-half of the Club and the entirety of Rafferty's Plumbing were no more, claimed by the raging Quinebaug. I remember standing and looking at that amazing sight of half of what used to be a sizeable building; I wondered about where the other half had gone and just what had gone with it. Never one to miss an opportunity to teach life lessons, Mom stood with us and slowly instructed: "I don't want you ever to forget what water can do!" And it was a 'life lesson' for we had crossed that river so many times and looked way down to its flowing waters (sometimes no more than trickles in summer) and never realized the hidden force and camouflaged power. Those images and that lesson stick with me yet. Small beginnings sometimes do, indeed, have disproportionally great endings!

As we walked what used to be our downtown area, much of it now either missing entirely or submerged, it became hard to remember with any accuracy just WHAT used to be WHERE. In the immediate aftermath, there was no business to be done. Transportation was stymied, and supplies could not be delivered. Without electricity, frozen goods melted and were either eaten-on-the run or spoiled in place. Meat and vegetables were given away before decay caught them. Supplies of water were scarce but cleverly and creatively produced. And after about three or four nights of supper-by-candlelight, when Dinty Moore and dog food seemed indistinguishable from one another, any semblance of charm or romance had made a hasty retreat from most tables. No telephones, no radio, no television, no newspapers, only word-of-mouth remained, with varying degrees of accuracy, and, from time to time, rumors and innuendoes would make their way into the pipeline of communication, with only a slight chance of refutation possible.

Much as I try, I remember no reports or stories of any kind of looting or of any sort of criminal activity at all. What often seems to be the first resort in calamities today was, apparently, the last resort in the summer of 1955. Everyone struggled, and most people looked for ways to help one another. Ralph Bradford, our neighbor, had a pick-up truck. He loaded it with fifty-gallon drums and went down to Lake Alexander, where we had a rented lot on the south shore. He backed the truck as far onto the lot as he could, and then we carried pails of water from the lake to the drums in the truck. This way, back home, we at least had water for flushing toilets if for nothing else. The US Army supplied potable water, and a quick dunk and soaping and rinse in the lake (between buckets of hoisted water) had to suffice for baths and showers. They were unusual days, unpredictable days, but, for the most part, days that would remain memorable not because of tragedy but rather because of kindness, helpfulness, neighborliness, in short, living as a genuine community of people.

Those post-flood days were variously described as 'grueling,' 'bone-wearying,' and 'long.' And they were all of that, but they were much more as well. While I stood there and contemplated the fate of the missing half-building, Dad was concentrating on the remaining halves of the city's life. I think it fair and accurate to say that Dad was 'at the top of his form.' Listening to Fire Chief George Harper, conferring with Civil Engineer Gil Perry, consoling the Giracas and the Goulets, negotiating with state bureaucrats, thanking the Army Corps of Engineers, and cajoling the National Guard, he seemed to live on adrenaline and challenge. He was Mayor, the leader, and God pity the well-intentioned one who tried to send him home! In the ensuing weeks, life once again took on the semblance of normality. School opened on time, business resumed (perhaps lamely initially!), and the endless string of meetings continued.

Out of those chaotic and frightening days of August, came some of Dad's proudest moments. Putnam had, in June of 1955, celebrated its centennial. The city had proudly proclaimed that it had had 'a great past,' and it promised an even 'greater future.' That prediction, at least to the naked eye, now seemed somewhat dubious, if not totally ludicrous. The city lay in ruins, and the pessimists' prognostications were gloomy at best. But, to Dad's way of thinking, they were looking at it all wrong! How could anyone be gloomy about the future of a place, which had suffered such destruction, yet which had lost not a single life? How could anyone be pessimistic about the future of a city, whose residents had supported and sustained one another so staunchly and so well!? How could anyone doubt an even greater future for a town that couldn't even spell d-e-f-e-a-t!? The nay-sayers existed, it's true, and Dad understood their less than positive feelings, but he could never join them. He knew Putnam and its people too well for that. His belief in his fellow Putnamites was strengthened at almost every turn. When he saw the Daughters of the Holy Spirit at Saint Mary's gathering bedding and clothing, preparing meals, and feeding the displaced; when he saw neighbors loading their trucks with fifty-gallon barrels and carrying water from nearby lakes;

each time that he heard the familiar 'Thank you, Monsieur le Mayor' from a resident of Rhodesville, he KNEW beyond all doubt, that he was right.

Putnam's past was great, and its future greatness was assured because of its people and their indomitable will to survive. He had shared thirty years of the city's first century, and he would live to share in the first thirty-four of the second, and never would he waver in his pride or his belief in Putnam's people…"Good People," as he would often call them. In an article written years later, Dad would choose to describe his fellow townspeople in 1955 with one word: MAGNIFICENT!

Sometime in 1952, a man rang the bell at the front door of our home on South Main Street. Now this in and of itself was strange because hardly ever did anyone come to the front door; everyone tended to end up at the back door, the kitchen door. Maybe it was my turn to answer the door, but I remember leaving the table in the kitchen and, after some fumbling with locks that rarely got touched, I opened the door to a man who distinctly resembled our recently deceased pastor, Monsignor John Charles Mathieu. The man was hoping to meet the Mayor, as had been suggested to him. He was looking to open a Ford dealership and garage in town; his name was Joe Mathieu. After making him comfortable in the front room, I rushed back to the table, eager to announce that Monsignor Mathieu's "somebody," who looked just like him, was in the front room, waiting to see the Mayor. Naturally, my youthful exuberance ran roughshod over the truth. It was complete news to Joe Mathieu that there ever was a Monsignor Mathieu, and, as far as he knew, there was no degree of relationship whatsoever between them. So much for relying on appearances!

Hailing from Winchendon, Massachusetts, Joe had indeed come to Putnam to establish its first Ford dealership, and quite accurately, it had been suggested to him that he make the acquaintance of His Honor. Always on the lookout for advancing Putnam's business fortunes, Dad was eager to hear the plans, to fan the fires of economic development, and increase job opportunities for the town. No one – certainly not the two who met that day for the first time – could have any inkling that a working relationship was being established and a firm foundation of friendship was being laid. Only in retrospect would that become clear; but the die was cast that day, and its roll would bring long-lasting success and personal fulfillment, as well as personal fondness, to both men.

Dad's years as a salesman and Sales Manager for Mathieu Ford were delightful years for him, allowing him to earn a living, all the while stirring the political pot. I've always had trouble seeing Dad as a salesman, especially as a car salesman. The world of mechanics was never his; the arena of the hard sell didn't seem typical of him; the stereotype of the unscrupulous huckster just didn't fit…at all. But he loved this job, and, by all accounts, he did well at it. In fact, Joe Mathieu, the franchise's founder, and managing owner considered John Dempsey 'the best salesman I ever had.' As with every new job, it seems, comes a new vocabulary, and this one was no exception. In short order, the rest of the Dempseys became conversant with terms like 'cream puff' (an excellent car), 'a clunker' ('a no way excellent car,' and 'a special car,' an automobile which required very specific, if not idiosyncratic, taste. Joe Mathieu's inherent kindness and understanding made it possible for Dad to keep his political hand actively involved, both in Putnam and in Hartford. And so, the Dempseys no longer piled into a Chevy. Instead, we were treated to a seemingly endless succession of 'demos' from the long and varied Ford line of products. There was one which I remember in particular. It was cream-colored and green, and I presume (or at least I hope) that Dad had bought it because in an election year both front doors were emblazoned with a gigantic shamrock and the DEMPSEY name. If Dad had not bought it, then surely it would have been destined for enumeration among the agency's 'special' cars.

What I think Dad loved best about the job at Mathieu Ford was that it necessitated his being with people just about all the time, whether with fellow staffers like Mr. McKenna, Roz Connolly, Dick Turcotte, Catherine Meehan, Emil Boutin, or Joe 'The Boss' himself or with the constant flow of potential customers. He enjoyed the conversation, and I think he got a genuine kick out of trying to match peoples' wants and needs with available automobiles. People responded to his openness and lack of subterfuge, and some people, or so they tell me now, long after the fact, even drove out to Putnam just to buy a Ford from him! Of course, from the historically safe distance of more than a few years, I have had to realize that if all of the people who have TOLD me that they had bought a car from him actually had DONE so, he would have been a Ford prodigy, destined for great things in Detroit…probably as a marketing guru! But what made him good at what he did so well probably couldn't be taught, and I somehow doubt that Detroit would have been impressed with his fundamental conviction that all people are essentially good and that you just have to look to find goodness. At least I haven't yet found such a chapter in Psychology and Business Today.

Although Dad's job at Mathieu Ford was the best job he had yet to have, it was by no means the only one. Until the day when he became the governor's Executive Aide, there had always been the necessity of a job, of whatever sort, in addition to whatever he might have been doing politically. I distinctly remember him working as a distributor for a manufacturer of fire-safety equipment, for a synthetic fiber maker, called American Glossite, for Chase Going Woodhouse, as her field representative, and for an interstate trucking firm. Earlier in life, he had worked in the Putnam Woolen Mill, where he had joined his father (and sometimes his mother) as a textile worker. A fact that never seemed to fail to impress people was that Dad held no academic or professional credentials. Many thought him to have been a lawyer in days gone by; others esteemed he must be a businessman. But one of the most startling things to have ever been written about him at the time of his death in 1989 (and I believe that it was in the New York Times no less!) was that, following his decision in 1970 not to seek re-election, the following year he then returned home, to Putnam, 'to his family's textile business.' Where this came from is anybody's guess. But it's hard not to smirk, just thinking of Dad's reaction to this post-mortem distortion. Family business! His parents would have laughed themselves silly at the very thought. A family of mill workers, the Dempseys certainly were. Mill owners? Not even close! It's equally hard not to wince at remembering the symbolism of cloth as it once was used at the Executive Residence, during the time of another occupant. It was when Dad was Lieutenant Governor, and some friends had been kidding about him becoming Governor someday. With seriousness, if not forethought, it is reported that someone cautioned Dad not to allow himself to get caught up in fantasy. "After all, we all know that Governors are cut from a different kind of cloth from yours." I guess he was thought to be OK to make cloth, but that his cloth was somehow less than gubernatorial standards. How wrong that estimation!

Not so very long ago, a friend of mine from childhood had written to me. "I'm glad that we share so much in common, especially our ethnic backgrounds. Of course, you were rich, and I was poor, but…" This gratuitous assumption that a Governor of Connecticut has to have come from a background of wealth is not, even now, unusual. People still express surprise, if not shock, that Dad was not a lawyer, was not a college graduate, was not financially comfortable, and was, in fact, an immigrant! And yet, these were exactly the areas in which Dad took greatest pride, not pride on a personal level, but pride in the community and state and country, which had made success possible, even for a man without profession, without post-secondary school education, and without a firm financial base. How he loved to regale visiting foreign students with the hypothetical question: Would it be possible in your country for an immigrant boy, who never got to go to college, who never had professional training, who never had a lot of money to become the Chief Executive? Without pausing for an answer (which was seldom forthcoming easily or quickly), he would explode with pride. "Well it's not only possible in this country but it also happened...for me. And that is what made and what still makes this country great. Opportunity, here, is for everyone! I hope that you'll remember that when you return home. America is still the 'land of opportunity.' I often wonder, and I too hope, that they did remember and that this remembrance rekindled hope for others. Nothing would make Dad happier.

In this country's current dilemma about immigrants and immigration, I wonder if it helps to recall the memory of one such who came here with very little, but who believed that this country gave him and his such great chance and hope, and who, at least in some folks' opinion, gave this country a good deal more than he received. I'd like to think that when the sanity, bred of kindness and truth and civility, finally returns to these shores, we will once again rejoice at being a 'country of immigrants,' a society of vigorous diversity, one nation forged from many. Dad would make that his prayer and give grateful thanks for its rebirth.

Remembering "990"

Dad and President Harry Truman

'990' is 990 Prospect Avenue, Hartford, Connecticut, the home, which Connecticut provides for its Governor and his or her family. The Connecticut State Register, the so-called Blue Book, calls it The Executive Residence and describes it as a 'Georgian Colonial in design…located on six beautifully landscaped acres…overlooking the city of Hartford. The furniture and decorations of the nineteen-room governor's residence are eighteenth-century originals and reproductions." Built in 1909 and originally the home of Dr. George C. F. Williams, who occupied it until 1933, the property was purchased by the State in 1943, and it was first occupied as the Governor's Residence by Governor Raymond E. Baldwin and his family in 1945. Large, imposing, somewhat formal and certainly elegant, the Residence became home to the Dempsey family in January of 1961. In its own way, the Residence would come to symbolize, in very physical terms, the multiple changes to which the new First Family would be introduced, a series of challenges that would affect each member in some ways and to varying degrees. It's so easy to write these words; it's so much more difficult to get behind them and to know, with any degree of exactness, the nature and the depth of those effects!

By Thanksgiving of 1960, John F. Kennedy had been elected President of the United States, and it was no secret that he was looking to Connecticut's Governor, Abraham Ribicoff, to play some role in the new administration. What that role would be was unclear, but what was clear was that Connecticut would have a new Governor, if and when the President-elect called. My memories of that Thanksgiving break from school are still vivid: Speculation about Cabinet posts, about possible timetables, about futures: His, theirs, ours. We thrilled at the possibilities, and we worried quietly about the realities. Our family had known only one geographical home since 1925. Was that now about to change? Temporarily? Permanently? By Christmas of that same year, things would be a lot clearer, and, at least some of the gnawing questions would be answered. We would be moving!

My grandmother had lived in the same rented mill house since about 1926. She was comfortable there; she had good neighbors; she was near to all that she needed; she was obviously settled, and she was in her eighty-first year of life. I remember the discussions or the snippets of discussions, between Mom and Dad, revolving around Nana and her future in the changing landscape. Clearly, no one would force her to move. After all, she had lived independently since her sister Kate's death in 1954. And any invitation to join forces with an established family of six would come as a tremendous change for her. While Mom and Dad discussed, and the four of us kids wondered, Nana simply decided. Dad wanted Mom to 'talk' to Nana, and Mom felt that Dad should 'talk' with HIS mother. One Sunday evening, Nana spoke up, ending any speculation. "The furniture is old, and there's not much worth saving, but if there's anything that ye'd want from Church Street, just say the word. I'll get Jim-The-Swapper to clear off the rest." And so the decision was made: Nana would be moving, along with all the rest of us, joining the adventure of relocation for only the fourth time in her lifetime. No fuss; no muss! Everyone was off the hook of having to 'talk to Nana' about her future, and so a silent sigh of relief was assumed. Dad had been clear throughout the weeks of uncertainty: He would not like to leave Nana behind in Putnam, but there was no way that he would not respect her eventual decision, even if it meant that she would stay behind. I'm sure that he was confident that Mom would be more successful in getting Nana to 'come around,' but that intervention would not now be needed, at least not in this case. One of the last things that I did before returning to school in January of 1961 was to give Nana a hand in disposing of some of her personal effects. To this day, I regret, increasingly bitterly, that I was not more persuasive or wilier. Together, Nana and I stood at the cinderblock fireplace in the backyard and systematically consigned to the flames family photographs, old letters and postcards, printed souvenirs of trips and adventures, papered memories of the past. What I wouldn't give today to have a gigantic box of all those treasured memories, links to the past, pieces of the roots from which we sprang! Her fear had been that 'these will mean nothing to anyone,' and so it was better to give them a decent end rather than a slow decay in a secondhand shop. I do understand her fear and her reverential desires; I just wish that I had been more foresighted!

My younger (I add this at my siblings' insistence!) brothers, John and Kevin, seemed to pose the fewest concerns. John was midway through his freshman year at Putnam High School, and Kevin was midway through the seventh grade at Saint Mary's School. For both, this mid-year displacement would mean entering new schools already in full swing for four months, and without knowing any other currently-enrolled students. The awesomeness of the unknown must have struck them from time to time, but they seemed unawed yet excited.

My sister, Margaret, the third of the four of us, was in eighth grade at Saint Mary's School, anticipating the long-awaited excitement and joy of graduation with the classmates, with whom she had shared these nine academic years. There was no easy way to persuade her that moving to Hartford would be an adventure. In actual fact, there was no way of persuading her to move. Period! She wanted to graduate with the rest of her class, and that was that! Mom relented, perhaps more reluctantly than Dad, and agreed that the 'deal,' which Margaret had hatched and struck with her best friend, Roberta Johnston, would be considered. "With nine kids already, what possible difference could one more make, Mary?" argued Loretta Johnston. "She can even help with the younger ones. What do you say? Can she stay?" I think Mom knew that she was beaten, but she wouldn't give up without one last proviso: Margaret, with or without Roberta in tow, would spend the weekends with the rest of her family in Hartford. It was a done deal! And everyone seemed to win…to some degree or other.

Since I had been a student at the seminary in Bloomfield since September of 1955, I was delighted with the family's move. For the first time in years, I would be quite literally minutes from home, and even though our 'free time' was restricted to two afternoons a week, I would be able to get home often and quickly. The move to Hartford offered me a closeness to home for the next four months, a closeness that I had not known for a long time, a closeness that I had badly missed.

Dad too had been a Hartford regular since January of 1955. His was the unenviable task of commuting from Putnam to Hartford each day. Surely, he wasn't going to miss those hundred miles, especially during the winter months. Now, he would be a matter of minutes from the office, and, by all reports, he wouldn't even have to drive himself, an arrangement to which he had become happily accustomed. He knew Hartford well by this time, and, for him, like Hemingway's Paris, home was a moveable feast. Wherever Mom and the rest of us were WAS home.

After a few initial mishaps, like taking the wrong stairs and ending up someplace she had never been before and where she shouldn't be now, Nana seemed to take everything in stride. Having her meals served to her at the table was a real role reversal. I think everyone in the family will remember the day when a staff member poured her a cup of tea. Nana peered at the cup then up at the attending staffer, then back down at the cup. The woman grew nervous and finally asked if there was something wrong. Without batting so much as an eye, Nana asked her: "Have you a ladder?"

Looking bewildered, the staffer asked: "A ladder? I don't understand."

"Well," opined Nana, "you'd need something to get down to the tea!" Blushing embarrassedly and trying to camouflage a guffaw, the woman proceeded to fill the cup with tea and then beat a hasty retreat into the pantry. Cups were henceforth filled, allowing just enough room for plenty of sugar and some milk. In response to the family's mounting mirth around the table, Nana affirmed: "We may have been poor, but we were never stingy with the tea!"

In response to several different concerns, Mom asked Nana's help with the small dog, whose name was Pal, and who resembled nothing so much as a miniature black Lab all his life. It was soon agreed that Nana would be in charge of assuring that Pal got a daily 'constitutional.' And so began a ritual, almost as sacred as Sunday Mass: Daily breakfast, morning prayers, and then, usually about 10:00 AM Nana and Pal took off on their daily trek along the sidewalks around The Residence. No wonder, it was made clear to us over time, that Nana was far better known in the neighborhood than almost any other resident of '990.' In good weather, she'd stop to chat with gardeners, lawn boys, homeowners, anyone who happened to be out and whose time permitted a brief chat. 'The lady with the little black dog' was often anonymous, but she was known, if not by name then surely by the daily presence and neighborly affability.

Mom's was a totally different story, one which few, if any, of us accurately read or understood. My mother is a small woman, described by some as petite, whose size totally belies her actual strength. I believe that we had all come to rely too readily upon, too heavily, and too assuredly on that strength. She was the mother of four, the sole manager and staffer of an eight-room home, an independent soul who, for years, walked to do the weekly shopping and then took a taxi home, loaded down with the week's groceries. Although not an especially social or gregarious person by nature, she had made the adjustments required of the wife of the mayor, the wife of a State Representative, and even the wife of the state's Lieutenant Governor. And in all these cases, she had remained anchored in the surety of her own home, surrounded closely by her own family, and in control of the daily life and happenings of her own home. Her strength had weathered a miscarriage, the deaths of her parents, the distance of her siblings, the nursing of her dying father-in-law, the care of two nephews, the loss of elections, the constant vagaries of political life, and the multitudes of daily 'crises' that are part and parcel of marriage and family life. But this change, this move would be totally different in its demands on her strength, and we didn't seem to realize that readily or well. Initially, the strains of the new and the unknown were understandable. She had to find schools for the boys, close and pack the Putnam house, help Nana to get organized, arrange for cancellations of services, and say good-byes to friends of more than twenty years. And the signs of strain were easily discernible. She lost weight; she slept poorly; she developed dark shadows under her eyes; her appetite fell off; she looked worried and preoccupied. She was busy, doubtless, but she was also preoccupied with a vision of the future that only she seemed able to see and fathom. Her strength was strained, but it was not, I am convinced, occasioned by the tasks at hand; there was something more, far more menacing than the throes of moving. Dad and the rest of us were variously preoccupied with our own endeavors and adjustments. Mom was left to wrestle this one on her own, at least for a while.

January 24, 1961, had been chosen as Inauguration Day. [Dad had actually and automatically become Governor by succession when Governor Ribicoff resigned on January 21st.] It was also a moving day for the family. Dad's one insistence was that the day begin with Mass at Saint Mary's, our parish church, in Putnam. Then it was off to Hartford. The fates augured a poor beginning. Casper, my sister's cat, was run over and killed during the night, on the street right in front of the house. But the day dawned nonetheless, and Mom was at its center, directing the movements, checking the clothing, inspecting the suitcases and boxes, and almost literally swimming in a now ill-fitting pink woolen suit.

In the late afternoon of that late January day, the Dempseys officially took up residence at 990 Prospect Avenue, Hartford. The house was generously staffed with full-time and part-time help: Butler, cook, maids, gardener, and handyman. Each staff member had a regular routine of responsibilities and chores, which assured the good maintenance and efficient operations of the house. They were sufficient, and they didn't need any additional assistance. Mom was to oversee the overall management of the house and make crucial decisions; the staff would do the rest. If she went to wash her clothes, someone interjected: "I'll do that for you." If she was caught dusting their bedroom or sitting room, someone lamented: "That's my job." If she visited the kitchen, she was clearly treated as a visitor, welcome to stay, but not for too long. If she told the boys to make their beds before heading off to school, someone complained about HOW they made them. If she insisted on having dinner at six instead of eight o'clock, comparisons were made with other prior occupants. If she wanted so much as a cup of coffee, she was invited to be seated in the library, where someone would be happy to serve her. In short, Mom was the proverbial 'fish out of water,' a housekeeper without a house to keep, a homemaker without a home to make, a cook without a kitchen, and a woman without a purpose. Over these initial months, we caught bits of conversation.

"What am I supposed to do all day?"

"I can't just read books all the time!"

"Why can't I do what I have always done?"

For the first time in my remembrance, Mom was not happy. I don't mean the occasional discouragement or the usual temporary disappointment; her residual strength seemed to have waned, and her usual, obvious satisfaction with life was no longer evident. A socialite she had never been, and she seemed not to incline in that direction. She had always done what she knew she did best, and in that she had found her satisfaction and her happiness. Now that very existence seemed threatened, and she bobbed like an anchor-less ship.

Dad saw and understood far more and better than the rest of us. He knew, perhaps intuitively, that the situation was serious, maybe even grave. If Mom was unhappy, then he was unhappy, and that was not how either of them had envisioned living their lives. Nothing could be worth that! Unknown to John Bailey, the Chairman of the Connecticut Democratic Party, and any, save a very few, Connecticut was close to losing its second Governor in months. I know that, at later telling of these events, many disbelieved the story, but I, for one, remain firmly convinced that Dad was ready, more than ready, to resign and to return home to Putnam and to the happiness, which there they had once known and treasured. Somewhere in those early months, a kind of bargain was struck. All decisions were put on hold. The family, as soon as the school year closed, would return to eastern Connecticut, to the cottage on Alexander's Lake. The family would return alone: No staff, no cook, no butler. Mom would again be in charge, at least for the months of summer, and then, in September a final decision would be made. And so, in June, we left Hartford for the lake. Dad once again commuted to Hartford each day, and, as he always did, he returned home each night. The summer and the lake were exactly the right tonic; he knew that for certain. But would that be enough?

In September, the family moved back to Hartford, and I moved on to Saint Bernard's Seminary in Rochester, NY. Mom and Dad drove with me to this new outpost, and somewhere along the way, I guess I must have said something to Mom, expressing my worries about her adjustment to The Residence and to the new life. A week or so later, I received a letter from Mom. "Also, Ed, you need not be concerned about me any longer, and I realize that you were, for which I am deeply sorry. It was stupid and childish of me to create another problem when Dad already had so many to contend with. But I have at last come to terms with myself and faced up to the fact that you can't just take the things that you enjoy and leave the rest. We must be willing to accept the responsibilities, as well as the pleasures, that go with this kind of life. And while I may not ever like some of the changes, I guess I'll just have to learn to tolerate them. But everything will turn out fine, I'm sure. So don't spend any of your time on worry about me. I'm fine; concentrate on you." THAT was typically Mary Frey Dempsey!

In some ways, this anecdote encapsulates the essence of my mother. She believed in the adage, "Put your head down, and keep going." She believed it, and she did it, and she expected her children to do the same! I distinctly remember the morning that Dad died when she said to Tim and to me: "This isn't what we wanted, but it's what we got." And understood: Put your head down, and keep going!

But for now, in the fall of 1961, the storm was past, and the future again glowed brightly. If Mom was happy then Dad was happy, and life could go on undisturbed.

The ten years that we would call The Residence home would be witness to a number of important family events: My sister and both brothers would get married 'out of that house' as the saying goes; I would be ordained a priest; Nana would breathe her last and 'go home' to stay; Margaret would return to wait out the last days of her first pregnancy and the arrival of the first grandchild; Mom and Dad would mark both the twenty-fifth and the thirtieth wedding anniversaries; and life would follow its inexorable cycle, leading us from adolescence to adulthood, from children to grandchildren, from First Family to ordinary citizens. After the initial hurdles had been cleared and necessary adjustments had been made, life on Prospect Avenue was really quite wonderful. The people of this state can and should be justly proud of the residence they furnish to their chief executive; it is a fine and gracious house. It remains the primary task of its residents to make it their home.

Although The Residence would play host to a number of famous visitors (among them Vivian Vance, Victor Borge, Danny Thomas, Senator Ted Kennedy, and President John Kennedy), it is not these occasions that have created and left the longest-lasting impressions. Rather, it was occasions on which very ordinary people did extraordinary things, and, thereby effected extraordinary impacts on both residents and guests.

Christmas may well have been Dad's favorite season of the entire year. Its annual warmth and conviviality invited forgetfulness of the rest of the year's problems and discords. The Residence was a perfect place for entertaining, and its spacious rooms dealt well with festive decorations. For years, it had been customary for the Governor and First Lady to host a number of Christmas Parties, for the office staff, the military staff, and the press corps. During the holiday season of the year, Mom and Dad usually visited the state's residential institutions, and they had been awed and moved by the residents of both Southbury and Mansfield State Training Schools (as they were euphemistically dubbed), homes to a significant number of Connecticut's citizens who lived with developmental disabilities (usually subsumed under the moniker of 'mental retardation'). Dad's inspiration one year was to change the venue, so to speak. Instead of only visiting these institutions, he and Mom wondered: Why not have the residents visit the Governor's home? And so, one Christmas season, after the remnants of dinner had been cleared, the assemblage was asked to sit back and enjoy a 'special treat,' one which, Dad suggested, might even touch them and remind them of this season's original significance and perennial message. An area was cleared, the piano was opened, and Ms. Di Leo and her choir rendered traditional carols and seasonal songs, while a tableau of the Nativity was created by other residents. To what appeared to be the utter amazement of the performers, the assembled journalists, photographers, and their mates rose to their feet, and with eyes considered by some to be extraordinarily 'moist,' they applauded opulently. Those who had lived, for years, in some of Connecticut's most shadowy regions, had at last found a new home of warm acceptance and hospitable welcome. Some years later, when the legislature and others would debate the relative merits of the Department of Mental Retardation's (today's Department of Developmental Disabilities') proposed Regional Centers, Dad would happily confide: "I knew I had the press on my side. Ever since that Christmas at The Residence, there was nothing that they wouldn't support for 'those kids.' We had won them over early, and their support was not the kind that you could ever buy, either politically or monetarily. They were the 'toughest crowd,' at least by reputation, and I knew that if we could convince them, their support would be invaluable. They had seen with their own eyes and hearts, and they WERE convinced." Since that first exposure at The Residence, some of Connecticut's people with developmental disabilities continued for years to leave their uniquely indelible mark on this state's Christmas season, and I can't help but feel that we are, all of us, the better for it.

Until his mother's death in 1967, six days after my sister's wedding and three weeks after my ordination, Dad would periodically express concern about Nana's adjustment to the 'new life' outside Putnam. If truth were to be told, Nana probably adjusted far better than most of the rest of the family. She settled into her new life and quarters with apparent ease and comfort. Her needs were relatively few, and her wants were relatively simple. With these more than adequately met, she seemed content walking Pal each day, snoozing in the library, under the protection of the outstretched Hartford Courant, wending her way through the recently-discovered intricacies of television's daytime 'soaps,' and feeling herself involved in the day-to-day dynamics of the surrounding family. The image, which she seemed to have of herself, was that of a woman who ate very little (despite what we all saw disappear from her plate), who slept very little (despite a constant rumble of snores coming from the other side of her door), and who prayed a good deal of the time (which she DID). Her oft-announced need for little sleep caused Dad some concern. The 1960s were not without their upheavals, some of which, at least occasionally, burgeoned into somewhat noisy demonstrations. One morning at breakfast, after a night during which a significant number of people had loudly and demonstrably visited The Residence, Dad tried to assess just what Nana had seen and heard during the night. Her room was at the north end of the front of the house, with the sweeping driveway directly below her window. His worry had been that she might have been awakened by the commotion, gotten up, and become fearful at the commotion below. Dad began probing gently, inquiring if she had had a good night. "The usual," she responded. "I don't sleep very well these days, but at my age, you don't need a lot of sleep." Dad pressed on, inquiring if there had been anything strange during the previous night. "Not at all," she rejoined, perhaps beginning to sense some kind of inquisition. "It was a lovely, quiet night, like all the rest of them. I was up and down, saying the rosary, and looking out at the street. It was lovely and quiet; nothing strange at all. Why do you ask?"

"No reason," said Dad, at last convinced that Nana 'didn't sleep' in exactly the same way that she 'didn't eat a thing all day.' He smiled at the other assembled breakfasters, confirming what the rest of the household long had guessed. The dead did not rest more soundly!

When the family had first arrived in January of 1961, Dad had asked for only one thing: That we all be happy in the new house on Prospect Avenue. Now, I know that 'happiness' may well be a very personally defined quality of life, but I believe that, for him at least, it translated into notions of harmony, freedom from stress, ease, and peace, within the confines of some kind of togetherness. To a much greater than lesser extent, I think he was successful in attaining his initial goal. However, he left there in January of 1971, acknowledging utter and unmitigated defeat in his efforts to convince Maureen, Theresa, and Annie (Residence staff members from Inishmaan, the Aran Islands) to taste 'spaghetti' or clams or roast beef rare! But, apart from that, we had succeeded in making The Residence a home, even if it were one which, proverbially true, we could never go to again.

In January of 1961, our parents had taken up residence at '990,' a relatively young family, with three teenagers, a grandmother, and a little black dog. They left, ten years later, just the two of them, for the first time in over thirty years. They had chosen to make their home at Mumford Cove, Groton, and it was there, at least according to Dad's telling that the full implications of a new and harsh reality would make themselves felt.

Dad would tell it this way: "You remember, in days gone by, as a newly-elected Pope was carried into his coronation, the procession would halt, and someone would appear before the Pontiff with a piece of burning flax and intone the solemn warning: 'Sic transit gloria mundi. So passes the glory of this world.'"

On the morning of January 6, 1971, the state's shiny black limousine, Official 1, picked us up in Groton for the trip to Hartford and the festivities of Governor Tom Meskill's inauguration. With salutes and 'Hail to the Chief,' we entered the capitol, for me, the last time as Connecticut's Chief Executive. Later that afternoon, we returned to Groton, this time in a State Police cruiser. That evening, just before we turned in for the night, Mom hollered to me: "Dad, don't forget to take out the garbage; they'll be here in the morning to collect it." Sic transit...

"Qui transtulit sustinet. He who transplants sustains." And so it was. The One who had overseen the original transplantation from Ireland to America, and who had guided the move from Putnam to Hartford, now sustained this latest transition. In peace and with genuine satisfaction, they settled into their new home for the next almost eighteen year.

Remembering A Public Servant

Blind girl asks to see what he looks like

Although Dad never shied away from the word *politician* (he believed that politics rightly described the interactions whenever two or more individuals met and exchanged ideas), and although he would be delighted to be designated a *statesman*, and despite the interpersonal skills that he sharply honed over the years, and which might qualify him to be considered a *diplomat*, I somehow feel that he would be most at home with and most gratified to be known as a *public servant*, that is 'a person holding a government

117

office or job by election or appointment, in service to the public.' Whether as Alderman or Mayor or State Representative, or Executive Aide, or Lieutenant Governor, or Governor, I sincerely doubt that he ever lost sight of what he believed to be fact, that is, that public office had very little to do with honorifics but had everything to do with service. In fact, I'd even go so far as to say that Dad considered public life his vocation – that into which he was called by God – and the purpose of which made no sense whatever apart from the notion of service to others, the public.

In a truly edifying overview of John Dempsey's life, the Connecticut State Historian, Dr. Walter Woodward, who studied my father's life and sought to unearth some possible reasons for what Dad did with and in his life, thought that some things that the young Irish lad saw and experienced touched him so profoundly as to become the seeds for later life decisions. In his talk, on the occasion of the one-hundredth anniversary of Dad's birth, the historian recounts the Dempsey family's initial attempt to emigrate to the United States. "After the final packing of suitcases, tearful farewells to friends and family, and more than a parting glance, the family had made its way to Cork and boarded one of these White Star Line ships for passage to America. This was in the summer of 1925. In 1970, as he neared the end of his governorship, Dempsey himself described what happened. 'We were actually aboard ship, ready to sail when a complication arose in the form of a demand for a much higher fee than we had been led to expect, for the health certificates we were required to have. Convinced and no doubt rightly so that an attempt was being made to victimize him, my father, a veteran of many years of army service, refused to pay. Instead, we disembarked, returned to our County Tipperary home in Cahir, and the ship sailed without us. Back in Cahir, my father got in touch with a civic leader of his acquaintance. The difficulty about the health certificate fee dissolved like magic, and ten days later we were on our way again, this time for good.' *(http://gratingthenutmeg.libsyn.com/podcast)*

Could it be, mused the historian, that the ten-year-old boy never forgot what power could do for good, for right, for the powerless? Was it then that Dad first experienced the wonder of power at the service of others, his very first taste of power serving the public? My sense is that the historian may well have been keenly accurate in his musing!

What has to have been one of the most backhanded compliments ever paid to my father came in a conversation a man had with my brother. After offering perfunctory condolences on Dad's recent death, the man launched into his assessment of Dad's years of service. "He really was one of the biggest fools I ever met. He could have made a fortune in those ten years, assuring himself a comfortable future. But, no! Not him! What a fool he was!" And that man is surely entitled to his assessment and opinion. I would simply yet firmly assure him that John Dempsey never had to regret his commitment to service, never had to tousle with a conflicted conscience, never had to apologize for wielding power for the sake of doing good, especially for those with the least clout. I had chosen, in 1967, as a kind of motto at the time of ordination, words written by another man with roots in County Tipperary's Cahir. Monsignor John Patrick Carroll-Abbing. At the close of his book, *But For The*

Grace of God, the Monsignor had penned: "The secret of happiness is to love, and the essence of love is to serve." Dad fundamentally, profoundly believed this, that service, especially to the most vulnerable, lies very close to the heart of love, and that love is the sure route that leads to happiness. So, fool or no fool, Dad lived a very happy life, fueled by love, expressed in service.

Roger Dove, who worked with Dad, initially in Governor Ribicoff's office, and who remained a friend through the years, once reminded me of a story that happened sometime in 1961. A man had secured an appointment with the newly-inaugurated Governor. Whatever he had wanted to discuss must have been deemed important to him because at some point the man pushed a paper bag in Dad's direction. The conversation then came to a resoundingly abrupt end when Dad opened the office door and announced for all to hear: "This man is leaving...and he won't be back!" According to Roger's story, the man had rested his case, sliding a paper bag across the desk, cash slightly appearing. Incensed at the mere implication, Dad had foisted the bag back in the cretin's direction, took him by the arm, and escorted him to the door. He was never again to be seen in the Executive Chambers! Roger contended that he had rarely seen Dad angry, but this surpassed anger; Dad was raging, and that fact was blatantly obvious to the entire staff. My hope is that the story made the inevitable rounds of the Capitol and that the visitor's possible imitators were smart enough to take clear and definite warning!

Dad was not a very complicated strategist; he was usually most content with getting down to the facts, unearthing the essentials, and then spending creative time finding suitable solutions. He never believed that he knew all the answers or even that he ultimately knew best. In this sense, he was the very humblest of men, honestly content with the truth of things. He made it a point to surround himself with people, whom he esteemed to be both competent and talented in the areas of expertise most needed by and most relevant to their specific jobs. I never remember him trying to second guess Commissioners; once assured that the opinion being offered was the individual's best, he challenged no further, acknowledging the competence that had merited the Commissioner's initial appointment. Rarely if ever did an advisor feel undercut or disparaged. More often, especially after a heated discussion and even more heated strategizing, the last remaining point was financing the proposed endeavor. And time after time, expressing his sincere appreciation to those gathered for their knowledge and expertise, and patient participation, he would look at their questioning faces and assure them: "You've done your job and done it well. Now it's up to me to find the funds! That's all for today. Thank you very much!" He believed in collegiality; he honored subsidiarity (the stance of allowing decisions to be made at the most local, appropriate level); he appreciated, valued, and respected competence. Some might be tempted to say that that made him a very good 'boss,' an effective administrator, and an authentic leader. He'd probably say that it was just 'good common sense.'

Both Mom and Dad had a particularly warm spot in their hearts for folks whose disabled lives challenged them and their families. Once, when asked, if they themselves had an other-abled child, Mom had quite spontaneously responded: "Yes; they're all OUR children." In that context, I'd like to hazard a guess at the inspiration for the Regional Centers of the Department of Mental Retardation (today's Department of Developmental Services). One Sunday, after Mass, Dad and I paid a visit to a Putnam family, who had asked the Mayor to stop by; they had a question or possible problem, and they sought his help. This mother and father, approaching their elder years, had a son with profound developmental disabilities. The son, now a middle-aged man, could do nothing for himself. The parents' question or problem lay in the future: what would happen to their son once they were no longer here or able to provide for his care? They knew of the state's institutions, but they had never seen them as a viable option for their boy.

On another occasion, when Dad was visiting a local doctor, he chanced to meet the doctor's son, a youngster with Down Syndrome. The doctor mentioned that ensuring suitable educational services was increasingly difficult locally. In time and after repeated reflection, once in the Governor's Office, Dad quizzed the pertinent Commissioner about 'local services' for the developmentally disabled, services which could be provided much nearer home, maybe some even provided on a non-residential basis. "Wouldn't it make sense," he queried, "to have those kids (and he always seemed to call them 'kids' regardless of their age!) go off on a bus in the morning and come home on the bus at night – like all the rest of the kids!" In due course, the Regional Centers were born, and services were moved closer to home, and when a Regional Center was designated for Putnam, you can be sure that telephone calls were placed, to a pair of aging parents and to a local physician. Their concerns had not been forgotten, and their questions were not ignored. It took time, and it took money, but it was the 'right thing to do.'

John Donne, the English cleric considered the pre-eminent representative of the metaphysical poets, wrote: "No man is an island, no man stands alone." And Dad was certainly no exception to that lyrical summation of the human state. If Mom was Dad's 'anchor' in life (and of that there can be no doubt whatsoever!), then he was doubly blessed, because in his public life for at least sixteen of those years, he had the inimitable talents of the gentlest buoy possible in the person of Eileen Dillon Bumster. 'Miss D' (as we were initially instructed to call her) had joined the Ribicoff administration as the Governor's secretary, a role she would continuously play until Dad's and her retirement in 1971. Eileen kept Dad on task, on time, and on top of situations. That is to say, Eileen was absolutely and quietly essential to life, in the office, out of the office, in life's entirety. If ever there was someone deemed indispensable, it was she. And never did anyone see her roiled or out-of-sorts or without an apt resource. From weddings to ordination to funerals, Eileen's was the first advice sought and, more often than not, the last word noted. Her philosophy and Dad's meshed wondrously, and the notion of service, especially of the oft-overlooked or forgotten, came first in her thoughts and considerations. If a cause needed to be pled, if a plight needed to be raised, if a possible clash were to be averted, everyone knew that Eileen's was the first door at which to knock. How many school teachers and their students 'snuck into' the

Governor's office for a 'quick visit' through Eileen's inner sanctum! How many legislators 'just happened' to be standing outside the office doors as the Governor exited, on his way to some gathering! How many times was the advice given to the seemingly bereft: "Call Eileen; if it can be done; she'll do it." If Dad's dedication was to 'public service,' his commitment was aided and abetted unstintingly by one Eileen Dillon Bumster. Eileen had come from a position as Dean of Women at a New Jersey college. After Dad retired, she took over the management of her husband's law practice in Wethersfield. She and Bill had married later in life than usual, and the announcement of her engagement prompted Dad and John Bailey, Democratic State Chairman, to invite the would-be groom out to lunch. I have it on very good authority that Bill was made to understand, very clearly, that should he ever, in any way, cause Miss D a moment's unhappiness, he would soon very much regret it! Nothing more needed saying!

Without the philosopher's penchant for distinctions, Dad was quite comfortable with seeing things as they presented themselves, as they appeared, as they were in everyday life. Whether it was to inaugurate a new legislative session or to dedicate a recently completed building, Dad saw the task at hand as being part and parcel of his job as Governor; they were simply different ways of doing the job, different ways of being the Governor. A Communion Breakfast in Greenwich or a wake in Danielson was as comfortably accommodated on his plate as the Annual Budget Message. The lines may have appeared to the outsider to blur, but to the man who saw politics as public service and public life as a vocation, the lines simply blended easily and unremarkably.

His ten years as Governor had been marked by a series of accomplishments, which remain, even to this day, fairly remarkable both in scope and in farsightedness: Several new departments had been created; post-secondary education had been significantly boosted; the foundations had been poured for the state's own medical-dental school; trend-setting legislation had been passed ensuring and safeguarding clean air and clean water; the courts were improved; new roads had been constructed; Connecticut had survived a constitutional crisis and the first revision of its constitution in one hundred and fifty years; the tiny state annually rivaled California in per capita income and in-state expenditures for education; and, in general, our state's reputation as a trendsetting, socially conscious, people-oriented place in which to live and work was unsullied, unscathed, a glowing example of what good government could do to foster and maintain a good living for its citizens.

The weight of nearly thirty-five years in public life took a toll, doubtless, and the understandable desire to spend more time with Mom was a realistic hope, but neither of these two things would have been sufficient cause for his decision not to seek re-election in 1970.

I was then and I remain convinced to this day that something else, something stronger and more powerful, something hard to verbalize was, in his mind, obviously afoot, and against this, he felt chilling powerlessness.

By the late 1960s, things had begun to change and even dramatically so. As Dad had been single-mindedly driven toward public life because it meant public service, a different philosophy, a different approach, and a different direction could be sensed. He recognized the scent, and he did not like it one bit. On the surface and for public consumption the story was that the time was right for a 'new generation' to have its day and for the past to seek its rightful place in history. It's hard to decide how best and yet fairly to describe what Dad detected as coming. In a casual conversation, remembered now only anecdotally, Dad assessed the situation in this way: "I've always seen public life as a wonderful opportunity, which I have been given, to try to do good, to help people, especially those who couldn't really help themselves. But now, I sense a very different perspective gaining ground, a perspective in which public life becomes an opportunity to benefit yourself, to get rather than to give, and that's just not for me, not for a single minute. Maybe I'm feeling like a dinosaur, who has had his day and must now get out of the way. In any case, things are changing, and the tide is with the change, and so I'll get out of its way, and hope to see it turn once again."

It's hard to describe changes that are essentially attitudinal and so unseen except in their sporadic incarnations. These changes could sometimes be heard in the words of younger legislators, whose vocabularies overflowed with 'me' and not 'them,' 'get' and not 'give,' 'take' and not 'return.' These changes existed in the stories, calling honest public servants 'fools' because they failed to benefit personally from their office. They could be sensed in the snickering when a governor vetoed a bill, which would have increased his own salary. They could be seen in the rolling of eyes as speaking fees were returned, with thanks for the generosity and the instruction to use the money for a good cause. They were manifest in the angry frustration of Democrats when their Governor called for bipartisanship and then telephoned the Republican State Chairman for advice and counsel. 'Talking a good talk' was fine, but 'walking a good walk' now apparently smacked of foolishness if not downright treason.

Perhaps it's a 'stretch,' perhaps not. Is it possible that as early as the late 1960s the shaggy head of 'libertarianism' was making an appearance? If, as a friend writes, "The essence of libertarianism (is) my economic self-interest trumps the rights of the group..." then Dad may have been well ahead of his time in recognizing and distancing himself roundly from this currently menacing philosophy of legal, political, financial laissez-faire. Self-interest, self-centeredness, self-aggrandizement, and selfishness were not human proclivities that attracted Dad. In fact, his draw and fascination were precisely the opposite. And that, as far as I can tell, was the baseline motivation for his decision not to seek or accept the gubernatorial nomination in 1970. He'd leave the field with his philosophy still intact, his integrity uncompromised, and his hope in a redirected future yet alive.

Remembering A Catholic-Christian Gentleman

Dad and his mom

Dad was an unabashed Christian 'of the Catholic sort,' and like his father before him, he subscribed to the genteel ways of yesteryear: stepping down from the sidewalk if Sisters were passing, reverently crossing himself as he passed a Catholic church, and having a mouth devoid of swearing, smut, and crassness. At times, I feel sure, this warranted a reputation as a 'goody two-shoes,' or being 'square,' or living in 'another world.' But if that were ever said in his hearing, I feel sure that he would have heard it as a distinct compliment. I never knew him to back down from his stance as either a Catholic Christian or a gentleman. And if, and rarely, in the heat of some discussion or disagreement, he 'slipped' and said something untoward, he was very quick to apologize for the aberrant behavior.

His was a faith that was as simple as it was strong. He was raised by parents whose Catholic faith was fundamentally part and parcel of life, a foundation on which all else was structured. In their small hometown, the activities of daily life revolved around Saint Mary's Church. The vast majority of people in Cahir were, like the Loobys and the Dempseys, members of that same parish. The first few years of schooling were at the hands of the local Sisters of Mercy. And even the local Boys' School bookended the day with prayer, as well as having Religion as an academic subject. When the trio settled in Putnam, CT, they traded one Saint Mary's parish for another.

Dad nostalgically recalled a very cold and snowy December 8, 1925, the patronal feast of their new country, the feast of the Immaculate Conception, a holy day of obligation, mandating attendance at Mass. By no means a public holiday, it was a regular workday for the adults and a school day for the kids. So, that meant Mass at six in the morning, a time that allowed Grampy promptness for the seven o'clock shift in the mill, and Dad to be on time for the opening school bell at Israel Putnam School. They lived some two miles from the church, and, like most of their fellows, the usual mode of transportation was 'the two feet God gave you.' It must have still been dark that morning as the trio topped the first hill from the house, and Dad was lagging behind. His father turned as if to reprimand the straggler, but found his ten-year boy in tears. Taken somewhat aback, Grampy asked Dad what was going on. The chilled boy responded: "Back home, in Cahir, the other kids told me that it gets so cold in America that little kids' ears fall right off them! And I think mine are just about to fall!"

His father silently removed the muffler from around his own neck, wrapped it around his son's head and ears, and tucking it into his coat, reassured him: "There now! You're grand." And the three continued the remaining miles to Mass.

Dad's formal religious education continued in the new country with the Sisters at 'catechism classes' on Saturday morning, and later, in his high school years, through the parish Catholic Youth Organization or CYO. Toward the end of those four high school years, their CYO mentor, Father John Wodarski, urged his young charges to form small study groups, which would meet on their own, apart from the larger formal weekly meetings. The study groups would do exactly that: Explore their religion together, puzzling together about how to live their faith in the day-to-day world. To the end of his days, Dad could proudly recall that his study group was called The Little Flower Group (named for the recently minted Saint Therese de Lisieux); he could then recite the names of a good few of his fellow members.[Parenthetically and somewhat cattily, my mother was sometimes known to wonder out loud 'just how much religion ever got studied' in those mixed-gender groups of teenagers!]

The 1930s were still part of an era when high school graduations featured a Baccalaureate Service, locally held each year at the Putnam Congregational Church. Needless to say, and conforming to the norms of that time, Dad and his fellow Catholics were not in attendance; their religion would not permit such fraternization. Years later, often when he was a guest speaker in a Protestant church, he would shamefacedly acknowledge the inherent bigotry of his earlier days, and then, in a near whisper, assure the listeners that "just because the Catholic kids weren't allowed to participate publicly, that didn't mean they didn't silently pray 'in absentia' along with their gathered classmates."

One of the great demarcations between Catholics and Protestants was the doxology at the close of the Lord's Prayer (i.e. For thine is the kingdom etc.), which was part and parcel of the Protestant prayer, but which was non-existent in the Catholic version. It was Dad's secretary, Eileen, who, years later, would comment: "Watch you father when it comes time for the Our Father." And sure enough, at the prayer's Catholic conclusion, Dad's voice would stop, but his silent lips kept praying along with the rest of the assembly. Diplomacy? More likely a simple faith in prayer, whatever the version!

For a number of years, Dad served as an usher and collector in the local Putnam parish. Sunday was an occasion to meet and greet folks you didn't see but on this occasion. To exchange news of the week, to get caught up on the sagas of daily life, and if you were so inclined, to bend a political ear or two. This was fine with Dad so long as the bending was done before or after Mass and NOT invasively during Mass. He took his responsibilities seriously but not so seriously that he couldn't kid or joke about it. One of his fellows, Johnny Briere, was extremely conscientious and serious. One Sunday, after Mass, as the ushers-collectors were shepherding the day's offerings into the safety of the sacristy, Dad said to Johnny conspiratorially, "You took your ten percent, right?" Poor Johnny began to remonstrate sputteringly and to assure Dad that he never touched the collection money. Dad quickly and reassuringly convinced Johnny that he was just 'joshing' him, but a lesson was learned: Never kid a serious guy about what he sees as a quasi-sacred duty. Never!

How many Sunday mornings, when the rest of us got up, Dad was already long gone, to celebrate Mass with some distant parish, whose men's retreat group or Holy Name Society or Knights of Columbus were having a Communion Breakfast, following Mass, to which Dad had been invited as guest speaker. Such occasions were usually at either 8:00 AM or 9:00 AM because the Catholic tradition and regulation at that time prescribed an absolute fast from the prior midnight. No food! No water! No nothing! And so, on an empty stomach, often in the morning's dark, he would drive to Harwinton or Sharon or Bridgeport or Greenwich. And his oft-shared advice to those gathered men. "If you want to give your families an example, then BE that example yourself. Set the example by being the example." Even now, many years after his death, I will sometimes run into someone who remembers those Communion Breakfasts and who can quote verbatim the advice given and received. He seems to have been effective!

Dad's religion demanded absolute respect for members of the clergy – all clergy – regardless of denomination. However, that respect did not disallow trumping dishonesty. One time, a local bishop made the very grave mistake of lying to Dad in a face-to-face confrontation. Dad listened, respectfully, and then, reaching into his breast pocket, produced a legal document categorically contradicting what the unwise cleric had just reiterated. As the prelate turned the color of his episcopal garb, Dad stood and leaned across the man's desk. "Don't... you...ever...lie...to me...again...Your Excellency. Thank you for your time. Say a prayer for me if you would; I need it." I'm not sure if those two paths ever crossed again, or if the two men ever again spoke, but somehow I feel assured that the errant hierarch never forgot that particular encounter with a loyal member of the flock, who 'called them as he saw them.'

This respect for the clergy sometimes raised dilemmas if not ethical conundrums. There were occasions when an ecclesiastical superior would seek his aid in 'helping' some errant cleric, stopped by police for exceeding the speed limit or driving without the presence of license and registration, or even aberrations of a more serious nature. If it were possible legally to 'help,' if he could reasonably and conscientiously intervene, he would. And when I asked him once about these kinds of situations, he recalled his one year spent at Providence College. There, he remembered, his Dominican mentors had often shared with the students the wisdom of one of their own, Thomas Aquinas. When someone had asked the saint what the ultimate determinant was for making a right or correct decision, he is said to have responded: "In the end, you must ask yourself but one question: Is it a loving action? If it is truly loving, then do it. If it isn't, then avoid it." In an uncomplicated way, I think Dad often reverted back to that wisdom and followed it.

No one in the Catholic community had a greater fondness for the Sisters than did Dad. His education had begun at Cahir's Mercy Convent; his religious formation continued with the Daughters of the Holy Spirit in Putnam, and his four children were all educated by that same community. Nothing made him happier than to make an annual visit to that Putnam convent, shortly before Christmas, armed with a sizeable box of Rock Cornish Game Hens, procured from his friend Jacques Makowsky's Idle Wild Farm in neighboring Pomfret. No visit would be complete without the unpacking of the birds from their boxes with dry ice and a short lecture on the inherent dangers of said material. Poor Sister Mary Alexandrine would then have to straight-facedly hear the annual lecture on just how to prepare said birds for Christmas (a process about which Dad knew absolutely nothing, except for what Mom had assiduously taught him to say!)

On another occasion, Dad had invited a group of Sisters of Saint Joseph of Chambery to the Residence. In the office, one of his staff had wondered out loud if the Sisters would be permitted to eat and or drink anything 'outside the convent.' Dad said nothing, but that evening he called his friend Bishop Hackett, a neighbor across the street. Dad described the proposed Tea at the Residence and asked if there were some prohibitions against the Sisters' partaking. The bishop, doubtless genially smiling, told Dad: "Tell the good Sisters that, for this occasion, I have personally dispensed them from any and all prohibitions against eating outside the convent confines." And so the event opened with Dad, extremely seriously, conveying to the assembled Women Religious, that they were free (and expected) to partake liberally of the fare to be served – which he himself had spent the entire previous evening preparing. The laughter was uproarious but kindly.

However, not all such encounters with women religious were warm and cordial. In the summer of 1965, on his first trip back to his hometown of Cahir in over thirty years, the local Sisters of Mercy invited him and his party to tea. The current superior, Mother Emmanuel, shared what she expected to be surprising news: One of Dad's teachers from primary school was still alive and in attendance. Mother Mercy, now in her nineties, was then wheeled forward and re-introduced to the former student. An accompanying newspaper writer from the Hartford Courant, Charlie Morse, pressed her for a reaction by first asking if she remembered young John. Nodding her head, she said that she did remember him. He then pushed on saying that he supposed that the Governor had been a stand-out student. Not missing a beat, the former teacher said: "I wouldn't say that!" Later that evening, Dad allowed as to how, despite her name, Mother Mercy never really understood the meaning of that word!

On that same trip back to Cahir, Dad had the great good fortune to make the acquaintance of Archdeacon Arthur Armstrong, the pastor of Saint Paul's, the local Church of Ireland parish. The Archdeacon had been part of the formal welcoming committee that July. He and his wife, Sarah, had invited us to their home for tea. The following summer, I was to be ordained to the diaconate at Saint Mary's, the local Catholic parish. Mom, Dad, and a contingent of family friends surreptitiously flew over in time for the ordination. Canon Harty, the local PP (Parish Priest or pastor) came to seek Dad's help. It seems that Archdeacon Armstrong, who along with his wife and daughter, Lesley, had been invited to the ordination, was fully intent on attending both the church service and the luncheon following. Dad was delighted with the news, but clearly, the Canon was not. As the ordination was to take place at 11:00 on Sunday morning, the Archdeacon had apparently decided to cancel services at Saint Paul's in order to attend. The Canon had argued but to no avail, that that would not be well seen or taken by the Church of Ireland parishioners. However, the Archdeacon remained firm. And so, the Canon was now asking Dad to intervene in order to keep peace and harmony in the town. Summoning his most highly polished diplomatic skills, Dad shared with the Archdeacon his admiration for King Solomon of old, whose wisdom had counseled him to cleave a baby in two so as to satisfy the demands of the two purported mothers. That, of course, would not have satisfied either party. "But," continued Dad, leaning conspiratorially into the Archdeacon, "sometimes half a loaf is better than a whole loaf, especially if the whole loaf would leave some folks hungry." The Archdeacon nodded in subtle agreement. He and Sarah and Lesley greeted us at the church doors, as the ordination ended, and joined us for the parade to Cahir House Hotel and a full afternoon of celebrating, where the Archdeacon gave the benediction. A respectful friendship was sealed that day, and I sometimes wonder how often the half loaf is indeed preferable to the whole. It rather reminds me of today's maxim about not sacrificing the good for the sake of the best!

Following in the wake of his parents, Dad was never shy about his religious beliefs and the traditions which sprang from that source. His conversation could be punctuated with 'God willing,' or 'please God,' or 'God bless.' His religious traditions and faith were very real and significant to him. And there was never any sense of 'religious trappings,' or of insincerity when it came to religion. And somewhere along the way, he had come to extend his deep respect for that faith and its traditions to other religious traditions as well. He never hesitated to make the sign of the cross when driving past a Catholic church. He never questioned the appropriateness of his sporting a yarmulke. He never hesitated to enter a Protestant church, whether as a worshipper or as a guest speaker, though he did have to catch himself from genuflecting when entering a pew! Rabbi Morris Silverman, the editor of <u>Sabbath and Festival Prayer Book</u>, autographed a gift copy of the book by writing: "To my good friend, Governor John Dempsey." And he was 'a good friend' to all religions, his own and any other with which he came to be acquainted. He was delighted to sign an annual proclamation, designating Good Friday as a day of prayer and fasting in the state of Connecticut. He was thrilled to stand as a godparent/sponsor for an adult colleague's baptism. He unabashedly referenced God in speeches, lectures, and letters. The thought never occurred to him that Sunday Mass was open to dispensation, except in the direst circumstance. He was never, to my knowledge, embarrassed by religion, nor was he ever shy to urge ever greater religious fervor and observance. He didn't only urge others to give example by being that example. He lived by what he preached; he gave example, good example, by being that example himself. For him, religion was living, the direction for the way to live your life. He meant that, and that's precisely what he did.

The dictionary says that 'wearing something on one's sleeve' means: "To express an <u>emotion</u>, <u>belief</u>, or <u>stance</u> overtly and make it an important part of one's public life." If that's the case, then it certainly would be accurate to say that Dad wore his religion on his sleeve. Certainly, it was not in an ostentatious way, and absolutely never in a way to draw attention to himself or to impress people. It was a simple matter of being himself. His faith was simple, in the sense of uncomplicated, and his approach to it was equally simple: Be who you are! Some may have found this an affectation; I can only hasten to assure anyone interested that affectation was never a feature of this man's life. He was humble, and by that, I mean that he was fundamentally honest with himself and about himself with others. Some of that he tried to instill in his children by reminding them that the same people whom you meet going up the ladder of life, you're bound to meet on the way down. He was, in today's lingo, transparent; he had few if any illusions about himself. And that foundational honesty or humility was a simple outgrowth of his religious faith, which taught him the basic understanding that all people are equal in the Creator's eyes. And this faith, this religious conviction was a firm part of who he was and how he behaved. His faith guided his life. And so, I believe it only fair and true to say that John Noel Dempsey was a Christian gentleman – of the Catholic sort! As Bishop Daniel Reilly (former Bishop of Norwich, and retired Bishop of Worcester wrote in the Four County Catholic, August 1989): "Proud of his heritage, Governor Dempsey never hesitated to show that he was a Catholic. His Catholic faith influenced and enriched his thinking and decisions in public life as he proposed and implemented programs and policies for the people of our state." But I hasten to add that there was nothing ostentatious about his religious faith, proud of it as he was. He showed his faith in his words, his actions, and his being, but never in a showy way. When a Catholic dies, it is not unusual to see him laid out with a rosary in his hands. Not so with Dad. The decision was made simply, on the basis of his life. Rarely was he seen with a rosary in his hand; almost never was he without one in his pocket. And so, he was buried. His faith was real and ran deep; it flowed through him and his life endlessly. But it was never brassy, never glitzy, never meant to razzle or dazzle. It was simply there, and it moved him. The Memorial Card, at the time of his death, declared his faith simply and succinctly: "God is good!" He believed that, and that's how he lived his life.

Remembering
A Man of Principle

Mom and Dad in retirement

Almost any dictionary will tell you that an apt definition of character is 'the mental and moral qualities distinctive to an individual.' That same dictionary could then tell you that a feature of one's character is the possession of something called principles, that is, 'fundamental truths or propositions that serve as the foundation for a system of belief or behavior or for a chain of reasoning.'

In today's marketplace, especially the political one, I doubt very much that saying someone is 'principled' is taken as much of a compliment. Rather, I'd hazard a guess that the term is considered tantamount to 'rigid,' or 'unbending,' or incapable of bipartisanship. Nothing could be farther from the definition as displayed in Dad's life. Maybe the better way to try to make this point is to cite a few examples of principles, which seemed to guide, direct, and structure his approach to politics and to life itself.

After meeting a neighbor, whose partner had recently died suddenly, the neighbor introduced me to their attorney, with whom he was meeting to discuss matters of the estate. The attorney and I shook hands, and he then inquired if I was somehow related to the late governor. With an affirmative response from me, the lawyer then launched into a series of stories from his own past as a youngster. He had an aunt and uncle who were notable Connecticut Republicans. In fact, at one time his uncle had been the chairman of the national Republican party. He remembered well how, on more than one occasion, a telephone call would be announced as 'It's the governor; for you.' And inevitably the conversation ran along the lines of the governor needing some advice or input from the head of the opposition. It might have been about pending legislation, the naming of members to a newly established commission, or how best to solve a particular problem. The lawyer said that this was nothing unusual; in fact, he remembered it as happening fairly often. 'Reaching across the aisle,' bipartisanship, mutuality, call it what you may, this was an approach that made total and complete sense to Dad. And so, quite logically, he used it and relied on it as a day-to-day tool in managing the affairs of the state. When asked about this openness to the political opposition, he said he had learned this lesson from his mentor, Chase Going Woodhouse, the local Congresswoman, for whom he had worked in the 1940s. She had demonstrated to him the insanity of refusing help or proffered ideas or needed skills; it made no sense to her to turn her back on something valued simply because the source was 'the Republican camp.' The principle of bipartisanship was then translated, in Dad's not unusual fashion, into a homespun maxim, like: "Remember: one hand washes the other!"

On another occasion, at a wake, the children of a former deputy commissioner took me aside and confided that their parents were forever indebted to Dad because when a Democratic governor had been elected, Dad had intervened and assured the new governor that this Republican deputy commissioner would do him no harm, had done a good job, and had a couple of boys in the seminary. The deputy commissioner retained his position and, as far as I can remember, retired from that post years later. Party affiliation never seemed to stand in the way of doing what Dad would esteem to be 'the right thing.' His administrations were consistently founded on choosing the best available folks, regardless of a political party. In his inaugural address on January 4, 1967, the Governor invited the assembled legislators to adopt a similar stance. "My welcome to you is extended equally to all two hundred and thirteen members of this General Assembly. We have two political parties represented here, but we have one state to serve, and I know that the desire to serve is as great among members of one party as among those of the other. I appeal then, for the cooperation of both parties. I welcome consultation with the leaders of each side of the aisle. To all of you, I pledge my fullest cooperation. The people do not want merely partisan programs from this General Assembly. They want Connecticut programs, and that is what I urge you to give them."

Some of the most heated discussions (not to say 'arguments') were over decisions to be made which had several possible ramifications. The state chairman of the Democratic Party, John Bailey, might urge caution about a pending matter because of 'the Catholic vote,' or 'the Black vote,' or 'the hit to the budget.' However, it seems to me that all such rationales eventually paled when compared with the ultimate question he would raise: "But what's the right thing to do?" The answer to that question, it seems to me, became the final evaluative consideration and the basis for the ultimate decision. Dad wasn't either foolish or a friend of Pollyanna. He was a practical man, a political animal, and a realist; he could weigh the pros and cons of a situation very pragmatically. But, when all was said and done, when all elements had been weighed, his final consideration was almost always the rightness of the matter. A plaque on his office desk may say it best of all: "Always do right. This will gratify some people and astonish the rest. Mark Twain."

He certainly knew full well that at times money could be tight. But faced with the understaffing of a state hospital or institution, the potential danger faced by law enforcement, or the retention of a 'piece of Connecticut history,' you could be pretty well sure that the decision would place people first and dollars second. The story has been told countless times about the seemingly necessary decision to cut funding for the Governor's Horse Guard or Foot Guard, and about Dad's going to bat for these groups, who traced their existence back to the days of the Revolutionary War. The amount needed was really infinitesimally small in comparison with the total budget, and the necessary dollars were found, and that piece of Connecticut history was preserved. And those guards paid their presumed debt in demonstrable loyalty until the time of his death and burial. And there is no greater or more moving testimony to this loyalty than a portion of a news video of the funeral procession from the church to the cemetery. Before the hearse is a member of the Governor's Foot Guard, a man of a certain age, whose physical dexterity made marching obviously painfully difficult. But there he was, marching ahead of the hearse, as his fellow guards lined the street, leading us to the final resting place, a final and moving tribute to 'the man who saved' them years ago.

Bill Walsh, one of the first community advocates for alcoholism as a physical medical illness used to regale me with tales of periodic visits to the Capitol to plead for the cause. Dad's understanding of the clinical aspects of this disease was limited, to put it mildly. But, after listening to the professional and the tales of lives saved and lives lost, he'd lean over and smilingly open the bottom drawer of his desk, assuring Bill that 'I'm sure we can find something in there to help!'

The bottom line, it seems to me, in case after case, was PEOPLE. People had to come first: Before political considerations, before financial considerations, before anything and everything else. No wonder he was deemed a 'people person,' 'the peoples' governor.'

"Try not to take things personally!" that was his advice to us, his children, but how mightily he had to struggle with that adage himself. When a friendly neighbor accepted the Republican nomination to oppose him or when a fellow Democrat tried to wrest a nomination from him, or an erstwhile friend publicly and vehemently opposed him, he, quite naturally, reacted. But, never then nor now, do I ever remember his reaction to be one of either resentment or revenge. Rather, he internalized the opposition and there salved the hurt, the pain inflicted. Dad was a sensitive person, a difficult characteristic to possess in the arena of the political fray. His feelings could be hurt, whether that was intended or otherwise, and you could sometimes almost see the emotional limp, and yet I never knew him to carry a grudge, or to seek to get even, or to inflict punishment on an offender. I really think that he sincerely did try to follow his own advice, not to take things personally, and when he failed it was in his own regard and not toward the other person. Abraham Lincoln's words in his second inaugural address, "With malice toward none, with charity for all…" found the true depth of meaning in Dad's approach to disagreement and dissent. I doubt that he ever truly hated anyone in this life, though he doubtless came to distrust some. In some ways, some people have thought him too 'soft,' too sensitive to have had a successful political career. Yet he undeniably did! I wonder if that success was premised on his ability not to take things personally outwardly, even as inwardly he paid a definite price.

In John's gospel, Jesus is said to have instructed his followers: "Love one another; as I have loved you, so you must love one another." (Jn. 13/34). In very many ways, Dad's approach to politics finds its roots in that gospel passage. It was as if he read those words and decided that politics would be the stage on which those words would take form and flesh. Remarkably, he loved politics, and he did so I believe, because for him 'politics is people.' And his love for Connecticut and its people became, over the years, a stunningly reciprocal adventure. An editorial, written at the time of his death in 1989, assessed that, "He was lovable. He loved the people of this state and they loved him back, as no other governor before or since…He translated love into social action. During his ten years in office, the developmentally disabled, the physically handicapped, and the mentally ill benefitted from his compassion. He stirred the state to provide a better life for its citizens through improved education, civil rights, clean air, clean water, conservation, and safe highways…Goodbye, John Dempsey. You loved us well." He was, I think it fair to say, a loving person.

If I had to choose one example, one exemplifying story of Dad's principled character, I would have to choose that told by Alan Olmstead [as recounted by Walter Woodward in his 2015 lecture, delivered in Cahir Castle, on the occasion of the town's celebrating the one-hundredth anniversary of Dad's birth and later retold in his 2020 book, *Creating Connecticut: Critical Moments That Shaped a Great State.* (Globe Pequot)

As background, and as I remember the story, Dad was to propose in his budget address to the General Assembly a request for increased funding for the Department of Mental Retardation (as it was called in the 1960s). He was convinced that he was facing an uphill climb; he would need support from outside the usual political process. He knew the press corps could be a 'tough as nails' bunch, but he also knew that beneath the surface there beat human hearts, hearts capable of being touched and moved. Each Christmas time, Mom and Dad had a series of holiday dinner parties, one of which was for the press and their guests. It was decided to make a strategic strike on this occasion. Dad sensed that if he could 'turn their hearts,' he'd have the allies and the support needed for the desired budget increase. And Dad was committed to that increase. Here's Dr. Woodward's recreation of the Olmstead story: "…one of the ways he showed the strength of his commitment was through an event that made some of those around him at the time, quite uncomfortable, at least at first. Alan Olmstead, a columnist for the Manchester, Connecticut, *Herald,* wrote about this event, and I will quote his column extensively because I think it communicates just how radical John Dempsey's commitment to those others would have preferred to put out of sight and forget about was a half-century ago."

"Olmsted had been invited to one of the traditional Christmas parties for the press held at the Governor's mansion. But this year, he noted, something new had been added. There was on the walls…a new display of art. And the art display, picture after picture, was art produced by inmates of state mental institutions. Some were perhaps elemental and hopeless artistically speaking, and some seemed very impressive…(but) we wouldn't know from art standards.

'Olmsted wrote,' "What we did notice was the extraordinary interest and pride with which Governor Dempsey and his first lady Mary Dempsey, display these paintings on their walls not merely for their visual interest, but for the fact that they have been produced by lives which, in another day and age, might have been considered hopelessly blank and lost. This represents a breakout from the closed-door policy of other days."

"There was, 'Olmsted continued,' at the Governor's parties, some of the expected food. And then there was dessert. Dessert was the presentation of a Christmas pageant acted and sung by inmates of the Mansfield State Training School. Governor Dempsey must have anticipated and felt the sudden drop in temperature of his holiday audience as he announced what we were about to encounter…He must have understood, too, that some of us, not zealous to see the less happy side of humanity, had great difficulty in looking toward the performers then presented to us. But we think the Governor knew also, that as the performance and presence of these fellow human beings continued, some of us might grow stronger, and be able to open our eyes and turn our heads, and we would be better for it. And certainly, he knew that to make us look at this, and…go beyond our sense of shock to a sense of gratitude and shared humanity was a fit and proper thing to do in a season named after Christmas."

"It is in the intensity of his regard for these unfortunates, 'Olmsted concluded,' in the passion of his determination… to promote every possible ounce of public responsibility for them and feeling with them, that John Dempsey, as man and governor, is going to leave his own very special mark on Connecticut."

And I truly believe he did leave just such a 'special mark' on our state! And, needless to say, the state's 'press' looked kindly on at least one particular portion of his next budget message.

If, as I would contend, John Dempsey was a man of character, a man of principles, then the major principles, as I see them, in his life were these: Mutuality or bipartisanship as a usual course; doing the right thing as the bottom line; always placing people as the first consideration; exercising charity to all and malice to none; being loving, and that means acting lovingly.

So, to those current cynics who may scoff at the very idea of a 'principled politician,' I can only say: Remember! Remember John Dempsey, and know that what used to be could once again be born anew!

Afterword

They don't make them like John Noel Dempsey anymore.

In an age as narcissistically self-centered, politically divided, media-manipulated, economically grasping, and ethically challenged as our own, a man or woman with John Dempsey's character, commitment to community, and passion to serve others through collaboration would, almost certainly, never enter the political arena. Or if, defying common sense and good judgement, they did elect to do so, he or she would undoubtedly be shunned by party as hopelessly naïve, or quickly re-educated in (and indelibly warped by) the trench warfare of contemporary politics and winner-takes-all government. It is hard to find a silver lining in such a "get-yours-first-and-at-any-cost" political environment, but if there is one, it is this: the politics of division and greed ultimately cannot succeed; a system of governance that seeks its own success by ignoring the needs and ideas of its opponents will ultimately crash under its own weight.

And when it does, John Noel Dempsey's life will provide a model for how to move forward, and Edward Dempsey's remembrance an instruction manual.

The joy and strength of this book has come first from its subject matter: a remembrance of a remarkable "Man Who Did Good;" and secondly, from Ed Dempsey's skill as a storyteller, and the unique perspective he gained as John Dempsey's eldest son and as a Catholic cleric. As oldest son, Dempsey has given us an inside view of how family shaped the life of a man for whom family was central to everything else; as cleric, Dempsey sees with the wisdom of a counselor who has gained a lifetime of insight into the human condition. The result has been a riveting story of an iconic Connecticut leader by an author who deeply loved his father, greatly admired the man, and had insightful understanding of the public servant.

Remembering John Noel Dempsey: A Man Who Did Good is a family story, a community story, and a lasting and important lesson in how government – in the hands of a person of exceptional character, unwavering integrity, and commitment to fair play and true service to the people – once worked, and might work again.

I will read it again. And again. For what it tells me about the past. And what it offers for the future.

– Walter W. Woodward
Connecticut State Historian emeritus